Ian —

for future success!

[handwritten signature]

Happily Ever After

Expert Advice for Achieving the
Retirement of Your Dreams

Compiled by
Lyn Fisher & Sydney LeBlanc

 Financial
Forum
Publishing

This publication is designed to provide accurate and authoritative information with regard to the subject matter covered. It is sold/distributed with the understanding the publisher and authors Lyn Fisher and Sydney LeBlanc are not engaged in rendering legal, accounting, investment or other professional services. Each chapter is expressly the opinion of that specific chapter's author.

Legal Disclaimer: The companies represented by the various chapters' authors featured in this book did not assist in the preparation of this report, and its accuracy and completeness are not guaranteed. The opinions of the authors are expressly their own, and not necessarily those of the individual firms or their affiliates. The material has been prepared, or is distributed, solely for informational purposes.

Copies of this book are available for purchase through:
Financial Forum Bookstore
http://www.ffbookstore.com
(tel) 435.750.0062

Discounts available for volume purchases.

Publisher
Financial Forum Publishing & Communications
(tel) 435.787.2900

Table of Contents

There are many books available on the topic of retirement planning, so why did we feel the need to do another? While other books focus on one or two elements of retirement planning and feature the opinions of a few experts, we believed a book that contained the advice of numerous industry experts in one place would provide a more comprehensive overview of the many financial facets of retirement planning. Hence, the creation of *Happily Ever After.*

This book would not have been possible without the invaluable contributions of the authors of its 14 chapters. All are extremely busy and skilled financial professionals who are engaged in providing retirement advice to their clients and/or educating the public on these important topics. All selflessly gave of their time and knowledge to provide us the practical and useful information included within. We are very appreciative of all their efforts, and the efforts of their team members and staffs who worked so diligently behind the scenes.

A sincere "thank you" to those who devoted their expertise, energy and talents to assist in copyediting, proofreading, layout and design of this project, including: Ron Brounes, Kent Kirby and Montgomery LeBlanc.

And, last but not least, a special thanks to the staff at Financial Forum Inc.—Alison Hobbs, Cami Miller and Rebecca Kirby, and to our family and friends for their support in bringing this book to fruition.

◆◆◆

It's Your Life

In his 2006 State of the Union address, President George W. Bush told his audience: "This year, the first of about 78 million baby boomers turn 60, including two of my dad's favorite people—me and President Clinton." Along with the current and former commanders-in-chief, three million Americans are soon turning 60, and ready to start planning the next stage of their lives.[1]

As these baby boomers approach their retirement years, many are perplexed by the numerous financial issues they face. And, with an unprecedented $14.5 trillion[2] sitting in retirement accounts, that's a lot of money to be concerned about. All too often, baby boomers find their retirement plans are unrealistic, if not impossible, given their financial circumstances. In a study they conducted in 2000, Mark Warshawsky and John Ameriks found that only about half of the households surveyed were on track to fully finance their retirement. The other half, however, are likely to run out of assets—15% are expected to reach retirement with no financial assets; 20% will run out of assets within a decade of retiring; another 10% within 20 years; and another 5% within 30 years. The study concluded that, on average, households would be able to fund 24 years of retirement, but the half who are not fully prepared will face an average of 19 years of unfunded living expenses, amounting to $300,000 (in 1992 dollars).[3]

With these statistics staring them in the face, boomers need to make some hard decisions about how to best finance their retirement years. Those who have retirement accounts need to understand the tax implications of each investment they own and how best to manage them so they will last a lifetime. They need to explore the options available to them as they pertain to estate planning and, possibly, establishing or donating to a charitable fund. Often, they are faced with the task of caring for parents who, themselves, have little or no retirement other than Social Security available to them. Boomers are searching for ways to overcome this and other financial hurdles, and to ensure their retirement is safe and secure.

No matter what the size of your nest egg, decisions made at this point in your life can affect the type of lifestyle you will have throughout your retirement years. So what does the future hold for you and other retirees?

A recent article[4] shows that baby boomers are likely to extend midlife well into what used to be considered "old age." They will continue work-

---

[1] Happy Birthday, Boomers, Magali Rheault, Kiplinger.com, May 31, 2006
[2] The U.S. Retirement Market, 2005, ICI Research Department, Investment Company Institute
[3] Retirement Study, Mark Warshawsky and John Ameriks, applied the Quicken Financial Planner program to data from an extensive set of survey respondents between the ages of 25 and 71, taking into account college expenses for dependents, housing wealth, expected retirement age, life expectancy, future Social Security and pension benefits, and a post-retirement drop in living expenses.
[4] Ascribe: the Public Interest Newswire, www.ascribe.com, December 15, 2004

ing longer and have responsibilities, such as paying for college or having children at home later in their lives. They also are likely to enjoy good health and remain "actively engaged" longer than previous generations. Without careful review and preparation, these and other issues may threaten their "happy" retirement.

Industry experts suggest there are three major areas boomers need to focus on as they enter retirement: financial planning, maintaining good health and keeping a strong social network. It's important to have all three elements in place to be successful in aging.

For the purposes of this book, we chose to focus on the financial aspects of your retirement. To do this, we invited some of the financial services industry's top experts to address retirement planning from A to Z. While many of these contributors work daily with baby boomers to help them achieve their retirement goals, others are acknowledged experts who speak on, and conduct research in, their area of expertise. However, they all have one thing in common. They are concerned with your future.

We hope this book will help you understand the many facets of retirement planning, and that you will implement the many useful tools necessary to achieve the retirement of your dreams. We recommend working with a highly skilled retirement planning specialist to guide you down your path.

Here's to living *Happily Ever After!*

Lyn Fisher

Sydney LeBlanc

It's Not Too Late:
Practical Steps
For Your Retirement

David Harris, Managing Director, Investments
Christopher Buccheri, VP, Investment Officer
Harris-Buccheri Wealth Management Group of
Wachovia Securities

Mention the word "retirement" and a multitude of visions immediately come to mind. Retirement should be as unique to each individual and their family as DNA is to each and every person. The *process* one uses to plan for retirement, however, should be much more systematic, much like the technique used to evaluate DNA.

This chapter will present a systematic process for evaluating retirement that can be used at any stage in the life cycle. It is a method to successfully plan for the optimal use of a family's resources both prior to and throughout retirement. While there is no "right way" to look at retirement planning, there are certain issues that must be addressed if a family wants to avoid the common pitfalls and mistakes too often experienced by retirees.

Retirement is like a feature film where you play all the parts. *You only get one chance to have a great retirement, so you need to make the most of it.* Carrying the old adage a bit further, you need to take responsibility and be accountable for your own actions and "retirement." You are the director of this production, the only problem is that, all too often, due to poor planning, the script is being written as the movie is being played. Your retirement becomes reality television with no guarantee of a fairytale ending.

To start on the path toward your goals, the first step in the process is to take a snapshot of where you are both financially and emotionally. The financial snapshot consists of detailing all your assets and liabilities on paper. This exercise will produce a document similar to the balance sheet of a company. No matter your stage in life, it is a good habit to periodically review your accumulated assets versus any debt. This inventory should include any employee/government benefits such as a pensions, 401(k)/403(b)/457 accounts, deferred compensation plans, Social Security benefits, etc. It is also useful to categorize the assets according to their intended use, current (usable now) versus deferred, as well as by their tax disposition, taxable versus tax deferred. By categorizing your assets and liabilities, it will be easier to understand how they relate to your emotional needs and goals.

From an emotional perspective, you need to have realistic expectations about where your current financial resources are relative to where you would like to be in retirement.

From an emotional perspective, you need to have realistic expectations about where your current financial resources are relative to where you would like to be in retirement. During retirement, do you want to own a beach house? Leave a large legacy and estate to heirs or to a favorite charity? Travel extensively? Support family members? Your ability to fulfill your goals and aspirations is a function of how well you plan and will largely dictate your happiness and peace of mind in retirement.

How Much Will You Need?

Once you have an accurate accounting of your current financial situation, the next step in the process is to develop a reasonable assessment of your retirement cash flow needs. In simple terms, how much income will you need in retirement? It is crucial that your assumptions be reasonable and conservative.

Typically, it is suggested that a family will need approximately 65-80 percent of their previous year's salary or income in retirement.[1] But generalizations such as this can often prove disastrous. For example, if one of your goals is to purchase a beach home at retirement, you would need to redeploy a significant amount of assets, assume a large amount of debt, or some combination of the two. In this case, using the general rule-of-thumb would leave your retirement significantly under-funded. In addition, many retirees experience a "honeymoon" phase where expenditures are front-loaded into the first few years of retirement. Catch-up vacations,

---
[1] Source: College of Financial Planning

excess travel and spending often occur, eventually settling into a more predictable pattern of retirement living. Consequently, we believe a more accurate, yet slightly more time-consuming way of determining your desired retirement income can be achieved by time-lining the first 10 years of your retirement on paper. This method requires that you honestly appraise your non-discretionary needs and your discretionary wants.

Once you establish a clear and accurate picture of your required retirement cash flow, the next step is to identify any shortfalls based on the financial snapshot taken earlier. When identified, a plan for funding the deficit can now be developed. Again, we must emphasize that any accumulation plan be both realistic and disciplined. For example, if a family earns $100,000 after paying taxes and contributing $20,000 to their company retirement plans, but wants $5,000,000 for retirement in 10 years with only $500,000 currently saved, assuming a hypothetical return of eight percent, they would need to save an additional $250,632 annually, a goal with zero change of success.

Also key to accumulating sufficient retirement assets is to select a target rate of return that is both achievable and acceptable based on your personal tolerance for risk. You need to understand how much a particular investment might lose beforehand. The wrong time to gauge your ability to accept risk is while you are experiencing the loss, a mistake too many investors make. You cannot expect to benefit from the often-quoted 10 percent historical long-term return of large company stocks without also being willing to accept a potential 18-20 percent or greater loss in any given year.

Funding Your Retirement

Once you determine an acceptable rate of return that accommodates your risk tolerance, an appropriate asset allocation may then be developed. People often underestimate the life expectancy of their own particular age group. This would suggest that, now more than ever, it is crucial to have a well-designed investment strategy, one that incorporates both growth and income components, and that could potentially fund 25 to 30 years of retirement.

Funding a 25- to 30-year retirement means that you have just exited the accumulation phase of your retirement planning and entered, perhaps the most difficult, most critical area of retirement planning, the distribution phase. Depending on the level of assets you accumulate, there are many appropriate methods of distribution. Many questions often arise in this area. How long will my assets last? Should I take income from my taxable or tax-deferred accounts first? Should I set aside my annual income requirement or fund as I go? Entire books could be written on this subject but none would prove more valuable than experience. This is one area where we strongly suggest that you seek competent, professional advice. We can tell you from experience that distributing assets is not simply accumulating assets in reverse, as some would suggest. The methodology, philosophy, and impact of risk are completely different.

In conjunction with your retirement planning, don't eliminate the possibility and benefits of part-time work. Unless it has been clearly established that there is a surplus of assets to fund your retirement, we would suggest that you consider working part time, at least for a while. Generally this provides the most effective method of overcoming any shortfalls from the accumulation phase. In addition, part-time work in the early years of retirement can help reduce the risk associated with negative returns when the sequence of return can adversely affect your retirement. A nonfinancial, equally important benefit of part-time employment is that it can provide a smoother psychological transition into retirement.

Healthcare and Other Concerns

One of the growing concerns of retirees is the escalation of healthcare costs. As a result, long-term care should be considered as part of a complete retirement plan. Approximately one in four people will require some form of long-term care services during their lifetime. Does that mean that everyone should purchase long-term care coverage? Not necessarily, but you should at least evaluate the option. Perhaps your family dynamics would allow other family members to help care for one another or perhaps the cost would jeopardize your current standard of living. For certain, long-term care is more affordable when purchased at younger ages and when affordable, it is always a bonus.

> While planning you should consider some protection strategies for your retirement income, or at least part of it, to reduce the risk of outliving your assets.

Another consideration facing retirees related to healthcare is the fact that, on average, better health has meant spending more years in retirement. More years in retirement places a larger burden on your retirement assets as they are required to generate income for longer periods of time. As mentioned earlier, spending 25 to 30 years in retirement is not an unrealistic assumption for most people. While planning you should consider some protection strategies for your retirement income, or at least a part of it, to reduce the risk of outliving your assets. Your retirement assets probably represent one of the largest, if not *the* largest, components of your net worth. In most cases, they are second only to your home. Protecting your retirement income via a fixed annuity product is an option that deserves attention.[2] You would not consider owning your home without insuring it, so why not consider protecting a portion of your retirement income as well.

Another alternative for generating retirement income, although less popular, would be to utilize the equity that you may have in your home. Many retirees struggle for income, yet never even consider using their home as a source of income. Home equity lines of credit as well as reverse mortgages can make a lot of sense.[3] The recent surge in real estate values only makes these options more appealing.

When undertaking your retirement planning, avoiding common mistakes can help increase your chance of success. Tapping your retirement savings too early and withdrawing too great a percentage of your assets are two mistakes that often derail retirement plans. Accessing your retirement funds before age 59½ subjects you to a complex, and often confusing, set of rules and exposes your assets to increased longevity risk. Likewise, withdraw too much and you also increase the risk of depleting your assets. You should plan to keep your withdrawal rate to a reasonable level—somewhere between four and five percent of your assets. Common sense dictates, the less you take, the longer your money is likely to last.

Evaluate and Adjust

The final step in planning for a

Retirement Distribution Options

It is absolutely crucial that you understand the available retirement distribution options and the rules that govern them. We see more mistakes made here than, perhaps, anywhere else. Once again, there is no substitute for experience, so this is another area where we suggest that you seek competent, professional help. For example, let's assume that you retire at age 56 from a publicly traded company and that you own a combination of company stock and mutual funds in your retirement account. What are your options for distribution? Most people are aware that you can roll money from your company retirement plan to an IRA. They also know that, typically, premature distributions (before age 59½) are subject to a 10% early withdrawal penalty in addition to taxes. Some options that are not as widely known include the ability to avoid the 10% premature withdrawal penalty by utilizing IRS rule 72(t) which permits substantially equal periodic payments. In addition, you may take advantage of the age-55 exception which would allow you to avoid the 10% penalty altogether, but only for those assets remaining in the plan. Finally, you may benefit from Net Unrealized Appreciation (NUA) which would permit you to roll your company stock into a non-IRA account, pay ordinary income tax on the stock's basis, with the difference between the basis and the fair market value (the net unrealized appreciation) taxed at long-term capital gains rates when sold, regardless of the holding period. Some of the strategies may seem straightforward, but the rules are not. One misstep and you may severely impact your entire retirement.

---

[2] Annuity products have certain limitations, risks and expenses and are not suitable for everyone. You should consult with a professional before making a decision on an annuity.

[3] Lending products have risks you should be aware of including the fact that failure to repay the loan, plus interest, could result in the loss of your home.

secure retirement is to continually monitor your progress and make adjustments as needed. Your retirement plan should be flexible enough to accommodate the unforeseen contingencies as life evolves. Be aware upfront that, regardless of your diligence in planning, unfortunate events can and do happen which may necessitate changes to your plan. Embrace this fact and make the most of it. It is a good idea to take an annual snapshot of your circumstances, your progress towards your goals, and adjust your savings and spending accordingly. Likewise, an annual review of your asset allocation and investment strategy will help maintain the optimal use of your retirement resources.

Retirement planning is one of the most rewarding and beneficial processes an individual or family can undertake. Since you may reasonably expect to spend 25 or even 30 years in retirement, it is also one of the most important. The burden of making your retirement vision a reality is increasingly falling on your shoulders, so please don't take this responsibility lightly. Take action now, regardless of whether you are currently retired, approaching retirement, or many years away. Seek competent, experienced advice where needed, enjoy the process, and most importantly—relax. With proper planning, your retirement can have a fairytale ending

❖❖❖

David Harris, Managing Director-Investments, Harris•Buccheri Wealth Management Group of Wachovia Securities, adheres to two key principles: putting his clients' interests first and providing exceptional personal service. With 24 years of experience, he has advised his clients through various stock and bond market cycles while helping them manage the risks and rewards of investing. David specializes in providing income strategies to retirees.

As an investment advisor with A.G. Edwards & Sons in Bel Air, David was a member of the prestigious Chairman's Council before forming the Harris•Buccheri Wealth Management Group of Wachovia Securities in 2000. He currently is a member of the Chairman's Circle of Excellence and the Premier Advisor Program. David earned an MBA in finance from Loyola College in Baltimore, Maryland, and he holds Series 7, 31, 63 and 65 registrations. In addition, he holds both real estate and real estate appraiser licenses. Active in his community, David serves as a board member of Harford United Charities and in various capacities for the March of Dimes, and United Way of Maryland.

 **Christopher J. Buccheri,** Vice President-Investments, has been helping individuals and businesses reach their financial and investment goals for more than 15 years. He specializes in creative retirement strategies and business retirement plans, both qualified and non-qualified. One of his core strengths is managing the sometimes difficult transition from wealth accumulation to wealth distribution.

Christopher served as an investment advisor with Merrill Lynch and A.G. Edwards & Sons before forming the Harris•Buccheri Wealth Management Group of Wachovia Securities. He is a lifetime member of the International Honors Society of Economics, and he earned dual bachelor's degrees in biology and economics and finance from the University of Maryland, Baltimore County. He currently holds Series 6, 7, 31, 63 and 65 registrations as well as the Certified Financial Planner™, CFP® designation. Active in his community, Christopher serves as a volunteer speaker for the Chesapeake Bay Foundation, chairman of the Immaculate Heart of Mary Faith Formation Committee and Parish Pastoral Council.

David Harris and Christopher Buccheri can be reached at Harris•Buccheri Wealth Management Group, 24 South Main Street, Bel Air, Maryland 21014; (tel) 410.399.8465 or 800.324.4712; (emails) david.harris@wachoviasec.com or christopher.buccheri@wachoviasec.com.

At Wachovia Securities, we understand that taxes play an important role in your comprehensive investment strategy. While this educational book is not intended to replace your discussions with your tax advisor, it may help you to comprehend the tax implications of your investments and plan tax efficiently going forward.

2.

The Cost of Retirement:
How Much Will You Need?

John Goott, CFP®, AIFA™
Daniel Goott, CFP®
Investec Advisory Group, L.P.

Once upon a time, employees spent much of their working years with the same company and 65 was considered the appropriate retirement age. As that milestone birthday approached, they were often greeted with a retirement dinner, a heartfelt speech by the boss, and an engraved gold watch congratulating them for their years of fine service. The company also rewarded them with a generous annual pension that helped compensate them for life in their twilight years. The government also assisted retirees through the U.S. Social Security system, which enabled them to enjoy an even more comfortable lifestyle. Even workers who had just been paying into the system for a few years received that guaranteed monthly benefit throughout the course of their retirement.

Of course, by 65 years of age, many of them were not nearly as active as they had been in the past and spent those remaining years rocking on the front porch and reminiscing about their "glory days." They passed their time playing bridge or shuffleboard and tried to be first in line for that early bird special at the neighborhood cafeteria. For most people, retirement meant less than 10 years of relative inactivity as life expectancy was much lower than it is today. Today's self-funded retirement plans like IRAs and 401(k)s to which employees contribute and assume personal responsibility for their future retirement needs were rarely needed. After all, employers and the government were more than generous in providing for a comfortable retirement.

Today's retirees are often younger and more active and are living far longer than generations of old. Because of their healthier lifestyles and current mortality expectations of approximately 85 years, they will have many more years to enjoy retirement and live life to its fullest as opposed to just dwelling on past memories. (Some are even jumping out of airplanes or flying on the Space Shuttle to celebrate milestone birthdays.) They are taking up new (often expensive) hobbies, traveling to exotic places across the globe, and investing in second homes or timeshares. They continue to spoil their kids and grandkids and often help contribute to major expenses like education and transportation. In many cases, the new retirement lifestyle becomes more expensive than the one they were accustomed to during their working years. New, and often unexpected expenses arise each day and, contrary to popular belief, very few pre-retirement costs actually go away.

The reality is that most new retirees have not spent the past 30 years with the same employers and few have a pension to replace that paycheck (and even fewer are receiving that gold watch). While they still receive monthly Social Security checks, the benefit no longer meets as much of their retirement needs as it once did. Moving forward, the system simply will not be able to maintain itself as fewer workers are supporting those retirees who are receiving the benefits. (Per the Social Security Administration, in 1950, 16.5 workers paid into the system for the benefit of each retiree; in 2003, that number had declined to 3.3 workers per retiree.) While this social safety net represented by Social Security will most likely exist in some fashion, individuals should become less dependent on that income stream as a primary retirement benefit. Hopefully, they have accumulated enough on their own through personal investments and their retirement plans such as company sponsored 401(k)s and will be able to afford their new lifestyles. After all, today's retirement can mean another 30 years of fun-filled activities and related expenses. Unfortunately, many find that their planning has been inadequate. The costs are greater than they ever anticipated, and retirement may actually mean a different (often low-paying) job or some consulting work on the side.

Life Expectancy
A 65-year-old individual today has a ...

	50% Chance of Living Beyond Age ...	25% Chance of Living Beyond Age...
Male	85	92
Female	88	94
One of a Couple	92	97

Source: American Society of Actuaries, 2000 Annuity Mortality Tables

An All-Too-Common Story: The Carefrees

Like many people, Mr. and Mrs. Carefree think that effective retirement planning means simply deferring a small portion of that periodic paycheck into a retirement account and watching those dollars grow (hopefully). They may look at those brokerage statements every so often, but have found the process less enjoyable since the dot.com boom went bust at the turn of the millennium. The Carefrees talk about how much fun they will have once they have more spare time to enjoy life. They accumulate travel guides and cruise magazines, upgrade to better golf clubs, and make room in their closets for new casual wardrobes.

And finally the big day arrives, that alarm goes off, and they realize they have nothing to do and nowhere to be. The travel agent's phone number moves up the speed dial; Mr. Carefree's golf scores start to go down quite quickly; the homeless shelters become beneficiaries of Mrs. Carefree's out-of-style work attire. Month by month, the expenses continue to roll in. That personal trainer is more than worth it. That big screen plasma TV makes watching ball games so much more enjoyable. Credit card bills move into record territories, though they don't mind because of the accumulating frequent flyer miles. Investment accounts start to dwindle as they spend more funds with each passing month. The slight market pullbacks exaggerate the downward moves on those balances, especially without those retirement plan contributions that ended with their last paychecks.

> The *Carefrees* think that effective retirement planning means simply deferring a small portion of that periodic paycheck into a retirement account and watching those dollars grow.

A year or two into retirement, the Carefrees begin to realize they are blowing through funds like there is no tomorrow; unfortunately, about 25 years' worth of tomorrows still remain. Though they realize that they need to make adjustments to their lifestyles, they simply are having too much fun and don't want the "Joneses" to find out that they can't really keep up with them after all. The money earmarked for their grandkids' education accounts is spent on more pressing personal luxuries. They try to cut back in ways that no one will notice and begin to watch those retirement accounts more closely. They even consider taking some more risk within their portfolios, hoping that the next "sure thing" is right around the corner.

Soon, the Carefrees understand that they cannot continue to spend this way. They are forced to re-evaluate life goals and reassess their priorities. They can no longer consider that second home in Colorado, and, in fact, can barely afford their current residence. Instead, they must scale back and determine just how to survive on a dwindling nest egg. They explore consulting work options, but find that their diminished skill sets do not qualify them for the ever-changing workplace. Oh sure, they will be able to restructure their lifestyles and live a "relatively" comfortable existence, but it will be neither easy nor satisfying. It sure did not need to turn out this way for the Carefrees.

So, Just What Will It Cost...YOU?

Every year, thousand upon thousands of Carefree families move into retirement without any clue about the associated costs. In fact, most have no idea what they are spending during their working years, but feel very little pressure because those paychecks arrive every two weeks like clockwork and they more than amply cover any and all expenses. They have not thought about the dreaded "B" word (budget) since that first child was born several decades earlier. Yet, they certainly have been giving considerable thought to country clubs and country cottages, fine dining and fine wines, ocean cruises and motor home cruisers.

Whether a Baby Boomer, Generation Xer, or new college graduate, all individuals should give some thought to retirement, how they would like to spend their "golden years" and the associated costs involved.

In reality, retirement planning entails far more than contributing to a 401(k) at work. Whether a Baby Boomer, Generation Xer, or new college graduate, all individuals should give some thought to retirement, how they would like to spend their "golden years" and the associated costs involved. While the 25-year-old can only dream about what life may bring in the next 30 to 40 years, those folks within five to 10 years of retirement should really be on the ball with a comprehensive plan. They should be drilling down on their goals, setting priorities, and quantifying their lifestyles. And there's no better time to start planning for the future than right now in the present.

Cash Flow Planning

Structuring a retirement cash flow analysis (sounds much better than a budget) is one very important exercise that all would-be retirees should embark upon as they begin to think about hanging up those business suits for good. Take the time to evaluate current spending patterns and actively track all expenses and income sources for at least a 12-month period. While many individuals initially scoff at such an exercise, invariably they are surprised to learn exactly where those hard-earned dollars are going each month. In fact, most can quickly make an adjustment or two once they have a better feel for the costs of their current lifestyles. Cable bills seem illogical when they realize they have not watched HBO in years. The second phone line makes little sense since the kids have moved out of the house long ago. The daily Starbucks sure hits the spot first thing in the morning, but can they really justify a $150 coffee tab each month?

> Today more and more retirees find themselves caring for aging parents or other relatives, some of whom are incurring significant expenses in nursing homes or assisted living facilities.

The cash flow analysis process also helps pinpoint those expenses that should go away at retirement. Many projections claim that the average retiree's cost of living decreases by 20-30 percent in the post-working years. In many cases, however, expenses actually increase, at least in those early years. The daily commute to work now becomes a daily commute to the country club (and green fees cost more than office parking). Travel and entertaining expenses for conferences and seminars are replaced by cruises and trips to Disneyworld with the grandkids. What workers save on business suits and briefcases, now is spent on bathing suits and suitcases. The kids may be grown and off the family payroll, though inevitably, major expenses arise and a small loan would prove helpful. Today more and more retirees find themselves caring for aging parents or other relatives, some of whom are incurring significant expenses in nursing homes or assisted living facilities.

In fact, many individuals today are part of the "sandwich generation." They continue to financially support their children who are preparing for life in the "real world," while also caring for their parents who no longer have the resources to cover their rapidly escalating expenses. More would-be-retirees should anticipate that their future lifestyles would cost every bit as much as their current ones, if not more. A recent Employee Benefit Research Institute study (July 2006) shows that retirement healthcare costs for a couple living to normal life expectancies (85-88 years) can exceed $295,000 inclusive of insurance premiums and actual out-of-pocket expenses.

In addition, what other types of insurance do they need? The aging demographics have exposed a major threat of dementia-related diseases like Alzheimer's. Moreover, it does not only affect old folks in their 80s and beyond. Since nursing homes can run upward of $200 a day for a private room, many people are considering long-term care (LTC) insurance in their 50s (and certainly by retirement). While the costs vary, like all insurance, it will be far cheaper the earlier it is attained (though they may be paying for it longer). Still, long-term care insurance can be quite expensive and this decision must be given a considerable amount of thought.

Finally, many grandparents are choosing to help their children fund college education expenses for their kids. College Board studies show that the average public and private university annual expenses are $16,000 and $32,000 respectively. However, this does not take into account additional costs of travel to and from the university for holidays, fraternity/sorority and other discretionary spending money. These additional expenses can increase your annual costs by 30-40 percent per year. Furthermore, education costs are escalating at an annual pace (about six percent) that exceeds the normal rate of inflation.

The income side of the cash flow analysis equation is actually much easier to track and project. Those payroll stubs depict the majority of the pre-retirement income, but unfortunately, few employers choose to continue paying their workers once they are no longer putting in a solid "nine to five." As retirement approaches, the benefits manager should provide a detailed analysis of any pension earned and the applicable distribution options. Those fortunate few who will be receiving a pension typically must compare the advantages of receiving a lump sum payment versus taking it as a periodic (monthly/annual) annuity.

For non-work related income, old tax returns and brokerage statements can help indicate how much investments are contributing through interest, dividends, and capital gains/losses from security sales. The government sends out an annual Social Security analysis that should prove to be relatively accurate in projecting future distributions once the retiree chooses to receive them. Like the pension decision, workers must weigh the benefits of taking less Social Security income earlier or holding out for a few years when the monthly distribution will be higher. Personal health, financial circumstances, and longevity in the family are key factors. Bear in mind, regardless of when the retiree chooses to receive that hard-earned benefit, the government will not contribute nearly enough income nor prove as effective as in generations past.

As far as other sources of income, inheritances are a possibility for some, though more than likely, retirees will be incurring costs of caring for elderly family members instead. In fact, a recent AARP study revealed that only 19 percent of baby boomers (individuals born between 1946 and 1964) have received any inheritance at all as of 2004. Those folks who believe they have such a windfall due to them at some point in the future would be best served discounting their expectations and projecting conservatively. Many retirees simply love working and, as mentioned earlier, will choose to continue generating some income by providing consulting services or serving in a part-time role with existing employers. They enjoy what they do and like the flexibility to perform projects as their retirement schedules permit. Plus, the added income stream is a nice bonus.

Projecting Retirement Cash Flow

Once would-be retirees have identified their current cash flow and started to anticipate the future, they should perform a side-by-side income versus expense comparison and attempt to project whether they will have sufficient resources to last throughout retirement. At this point, their investments should be incorporated into the equation. Hopefully, these accounts have served their purposes and grown through their working years. After all, once the paychecks end, these funds often provide the lion's share of revenue to meet future lifestyle expenses.

As retirement approaches, some people choose to reevaluate their goals and tolerance for risk and rebalance portfolios to better meet income needs. Oftentimes, about five years out, they will restructure their investments from growth accumulation mode to preservation or income mode. Others believe this approach to be outdated and more consistent with generations of the past. Since these portfolios help fund retirement for 30-plus years in many cases, most individuals cannot afford to become too conservative. In most cases, at least a good portion of these investments should remain in growth-oriented securities.

When projecting the long-term portfolio growth, would-be-retirees would be well-advised to conservatively estimate expected returns.

When projecting the long-term portfolio growth, would-be-retirees would be well-advised to conservatively estimate expected returns. While many portfolios earned high double-digit yields in the late 90s, they may have struggled in the more bearish times that followed. Use historical total returns only as a guide for projecting future performance, recognizing that "past performance is no guarantee of future results."

The comprehensive analysis should depict the retirees' annual cash flow projections and show how the investment accounts will be impacted over time. Every six months (or on a predetermined periodic basis), distribute assets from these accounts to a risk-free account to meet the imminent cash flow needs. Do not forget to project for inflation within this analysis. After all, annual recurring expenses of $100,000 today will be much higher five, 10 or 20 years in the future.

Additional distributions from the investment accounts may be required to accommodate cashflow needs in those years with major expenditures.

Additionally, the non-recurring income sources and expenses must always be incorporated into the projected calculations. For example, key corporate execs may sell off certain shares of stock in the years following retirement. Those proceeds should be included in those pertinent years under the income column. Further, most people plan to buy a new car every few years and some still have some education expenses for that child just entering law school. While these costs will not be ongoing throughout retirement, they must be included in the appropriate years to be considered in the analysis. In such cases, additional distributions from the investment accounts may be required to accommodate cashflow needs in those years with major expenditures.

Certainly, the more detailed this analysis the better. Healthcare costs, more extravagant vacations, and new expensive hobbies should find their ways into these projections. More retirees are investing in second homes or even timeshares. If applicable, estimate and include these costs (even if considered investments) in the cashflow analysis as well. (Though the costs will vary greatly based on a variety of factors, an American Resort Development Association (ARDA) survey indicated that in 2004, the average price of a timeshare was about $16,000 per week.)

With life expectancies seemingly increasing with each passing year, run this analysis far enough out into the future. More individuals are living into their 90s and beyond. Bear in mind, cashflow will most likely change as people age. Furthermore, the crystal ball becomes quite cloudy projecting out for 20 or 30 years into the future. Often, those expensive hobbies are replaced with long-term care expenses. For that reason, most retirees would be well-served updating this analysis every year or so to make sure they are still on track.

Interpret the Results and Adjust Accordingly

Hopefully, the cashflow analysis will yield favorable results and the would-be retirees project to have more than sufficient resources throughout their lifetimes. To play it safe, they should stress test certain variables (inflation rate, performance returns, life expectancy, etc.) to ensure that the results continue to look good under different scenarios. If so, they have a few decisions to make, all of which are actually quite positive. They can begin to focus on estate planning goals and determine how to distribute any remaining assets after they are gone. Perhaps they want to provide for children and other relatives. Maybe, they have a philanthropic spirit and desire to leave a legacy to religious entities or charitable causes. Or maybe, a little well-deserved greed and selfishness sets in and they decide to increase their lifestyles a tad and incur additional expenses during retirement. Re-adjust those spreadsheets to account for the increased cashflow that is needed to accommodate these new goals. If the results remain favorable, go for it and live life to its fullest.

For many folks, however, the analysis will not prove quite as positive and their resources may not be projected to last as long as desired. No one ever wants to take the chance that they will run out of money during their lifetimes. While some people may choose to rerun the numbers and change certain projections, be careful not to be fooled into believing the situation appears better than it really is. Conservative projections typically pay off in the end. Better to be cautious at 60 than to run out of money at 80. With proper planning and the help of a trusted financial advisor, would-be retirees can begin to make some lifestyle adjustments early enough to make a difference.

Perhaps they need to reevaluate certain goals and find ways to cut back expenses. Maybe the dream of a second home in Colorado can be traded in for a smaller place in the country? While it is a lovely gesture to help fund grandchildren's college education, they should think very hard about taking on a post-retirement job to fulfill that goal. And don't even consider limiting certain health insurance benefits merely to save a buck or two in premiums. Additionally, retirement is not the time to take on undue risk in the investment portfolios. Should the cashflow projections prove to look less than favorable, simply moving investment dollars into more risky asset classes will most likely be a bad idea. The spreadsheets on page 18 depict Mr. & Mrs. Carefree's estimated annual cash flow over a 30-year retirement.

| | | Mr. & Mrs. Carefree | | | | | | |
| | | Retirement Cash Flow | | | | | | |

| | INCOME | | | | EXPENSES | | NET | PORTFOLIO |
| | | Pensions/ | 8% Portfolio Growth & Income | | | Estimated | CASH | ENDING |
Age	Social Sec. *	Wages/ Other	Retirement Accounts	Personal Accounts	Living Expenses *	Taxes Due	FLOW	BALANCE
61	-	-	-	-	-	-	-	2,891,000
62	16,848	97,000	118,080	113,200	(150,000)	(71,847)	123,281	3,014,281
63	17,353	72,000	127,526	113,616	(154,500)	(69,937)	106,058	3,120,339
64	17,874	47,000	137,728	111,899	(159,135)	(57,438)	97,928	3,218,267
65	18,410	47,000	148,747	108,715	(163,909)	(58,074)	100,889	3,319,156
66	18,963	47,000	160,646	104,886	(168,826)	(57,734)	104,935	3,424,091
67	19,531	47,000	173,498	100,429	(173,891)	(57,230)	109,337	3,533,428
68	20,117	47,000	187,378	95,296	(179,108)	(56,636)	114,047	3,647,475
69	20,721	47,000	202,368	89,430	(184,481)	(55,973)	119,065	3,766,540
70	21,343	47,000	218,558	82,766	(190,016)	(55,276)	124,375	3,890,915
71	21,983	47,000	236,042	75,231	(195,716)	(91,925)	92,615	3,983,530
86	34,249	47,000	349,136	49,040	(304,919)	(162,591)	11,915	4,989,121
87	35,276	47,000	350,415	48,714	(314,067)	(169,812)	(2,474)	4,986,647
88	36,334	47,000	350,189	48,742	(323,489)	(182,587)	(23,811)	4,962,835
89	37,424	47,000	348,527	48,499	(333,193)	(185,031)	(36,774)	4,926,061
90	38,547	47,000	345,011	49,074	(343,189)	(192,941)	(56,498)	4,869,564

* Social security and living expenses are adjusted on an assumed inflation rate of 3% annually.

| | | Mr. & Mrs. Carefree | | | | | | |
| | | Retirement Cash Flow | | | | | | |

| | INCOME | | | | EXPENSES | | NET | PORTFOLIO |
| | | Pensions/ | 6% Portfolio Growth & Income | | | Estimated | CASH | ENDING |
Age	Social Sec. *	Wages/ Other	Retirement Accounts	Personal Accounts	Living Expenses *	Taxes Due	FLOW	BALANCE
61	-	-	-	-	-	-	-	2,891,000
62	16,848	97,000	88,560	84,900	(150,000)	(62,791)	74,517	2,965,517
63	17,353	72,000	93,874	84,057	(154,500)	(55,702)	57,082	3,022,599
64	17,874	47,000	99,506	81,850	(159,135)	(48,848)	38,247	3,060,846
65	18,410	47,000	105,476	78,174	(163,909)	(49,742)	35,409	3,096,255
66	18,963	47,000	111,805	73,970	(168,826)	(49,409)	33,503	3,129,758
67	19,531	47,000	118,513	69,272	(173,891)	(48,976)	31,449	3,161,206
68	20,117	47,000	125,624	64,048	(179,108)	(48,561)	29,120	3,190,326
69	20,721	47,000	133,161	58,258	(184,481)	(48,223)	26,436	3,216,761
70	21,343	47,000	141,151	51,855	(190,016)	(48,062)	23,271	3,240,032
71	21,983	47,000	149,620	44,782	(195,716)	(79,793)	(12,124)	3,227,908
86	34,249	47,000	100,638	-	(304,919)	(170,234)	(293,266)	1,384,040
87	35,276	47,000	83,042	-	(314,067)	(175,519)	(324,268)	1,059,772
88	36,334	47,000	63,586	-	(323,489)	(180,962)	(357,531)	702,241
89	37,424	47,000	42,134	-	(333,193)	(186,569)	(393,204)	309,036
90	38,547	47,000	18,542	-	(343,189)	(153,174)	(392,274)	(83,238)

* Social security and living expenses are adjusted on an assumed inflation rate of 3% annually.

Initial Analysis (top chart): During those years, the Carefrees will receive income in the form of social security and an annual pension, which includes additional wages in the first two years of retirement. Their investment portfolios (cumulative balance depicted in the far right column) are projected to earn 8% per annum. They will also incur living expenses (beginning at $150,000/yr) that increase by an annual 3% inflation rate and will pay appropriate taxes. Under this scenario, the Carefrees will be able to maintain a very comfortable lifestyle throughout retirement. Their portfolios will increase over time and they will have resources to leave to family members, charities, or other relevant causes.

Stress-Tested Analysis (bottom chart): The advisor then chooses to rerun the analysis assuming the portfolios were invested in a more conservative manner and were projected to earn only 6% per annum (instead of a return of 8% as depicted in the original). Under this scenario, the Carefrees will begin to see their portfolio balances decline during retirement and will ultimately be depleted at age 90. If it is determined that the 6% projected return is more accurate, the Carefrees may have to reevaluate living expenses later in retirement to ensure they do not run out of money.

The Carefrees Revisited

Fortunately, the Carefrees actually had the foresight to sit down with their financial advisor a few years prior to retirement. They discussed goals and priorities and put together a comprehensive cashflow analysis to learn just where they stood on the road to a successful retirement. With a few years to plan, the Carefrees were able to reevaluate their current expenses, project the anticipated new costs expected in retirement, analyze their future income stream, and determine the appropriate allocation within their investment accounts. A minor tweak here ... a slight adjustment there ... and the Carefrees are now living a quite comfortable lifestyle without the stress of trying to "keep up with those Joneses."

> The Carefrees were able to reevaluate their current expenses, project the anticipated new costs expected in retirement, analyze their future income stream, and determine the appropriate allocation within their investment accounts.

◆◆◆

Did You Know?

Education: Did you know?[1]

• The 2005-06 national average cost for a four-year public college or university is $15,566 per year; for a four-year private college or university it is $31,916 per year (and does NOT include certain travel and discretionary expenses).

• The average cost increase over the last five years has been about six to seven percent per year.

Healthcare: Did you know?[2]

• A couple, both age 65, today living to average life expectancy could need as much as $295,000 to cover premiums for health insurance coverage and out-of-pocket expenses during retirement.

• A couple who lives to age 95 could need as a much as $550,000.

Vacations: Did you know?[3]

• In 2004, the average price of a timeshare week was $15,789.

• In calculating the total cost of a timeshare or vacation plan, include mortgage payments and expenses, like travel costs, annual maintenance fees and taxes, closing costs, broker commissions, and finance charges.

Long Term Care: Did you know?[4]

• In 2006…the average annual cost for a private one-bedroom unit in an assisted living facility was $32,294.

• The combined average hourly rate for a home health aide for in-home long term care was $25.32 per hour.

• The average annual cost for a private room in a nursing home was $70,912.

[1] The College Board, Trends In College Pricing 2005
[2] Employee Benefit Research Institute (July 2006)
[3] American Resort Development Assoc. - US Industry Snapshot (2004)
[4] Genworth Financial's annual "Cost of Care" survey.

President/CEO of Investec Advisory Group, L.P., an SEC registered investment advisory firm, **John Goott**, CFP®, AIFA™ brings four decades of comprehensive wealth management and financial planning services to affluent individuals and their families. These services include investment management consulting, retirement income and cash flow planning, estate planning and risk management strategies. John also provides fiduciary care and investment management services to the trustees of qualified retirement plans, trusts, and foundations. He serves as President of Investec Asset Management Group, Inc., that specializes in life, disability, and long-term care insurance, and Financial Paradigms, Inc., a limited Broker/Dealer and member NASD.

John earned his Certified Financial Planner (CFP) designation through the College of Financial Planning in Denver and his designation as an Accredited Investment Fiduciary Auditory (AIFA™) through the Katz Business School at the University of Pittsburgh. John was awarded the DALBAR Financial Professional Seal, a national award that recognizes financial professionals who have achieved overall excellence in the areas of client trust, financial results, and quality of advice and client satisfaction. His professional licenses include life and health insurance as well as the Series 7, 24 and 63 securities licenses. John is very active and serves on the boards and key committees of several professional and community organizations.

John Goott, Daniel Goott

Daniel Goott, CFP®, Vice President, joined Investec Advisory Group, L.P. in 2003. Previously he worked as a financial advisor with Prudential Financial in their San Diego and Los Angeles offices. As a financial advisor at Investec, Daniel provides wealth management services to affluent individuals and their families. These services include investment management consulting, retirement income, estate, and education planning and risk management strategies.

Daniel is a Certified Financial Planner™ professional, a national member of the Financial Planning Association and is active in its local Houston chapter. Held to the strict guidelines of the Certified Financial Planner Board of Standards, Daniel assumes a fiduciary role with his clients. Daniel earned his Bachelors of Business Administration degree from the University of Texas with a concentration in Finance. His professional licenses include life and health insurance as well as the Series 7, 28, 63 and 65 securities licenses. He also serves as the Financial and Operations Principal of Financial Paradigms, Inc., a limited broker/dealer, member NASD.

John or Daniel can be reached at Investec Advisory Group L.P., 1001 West Loop South, Ste. 800, Houston, Texas 77027; (tel) 713.622.9111 or 800.380.1578; (email) daniel@investec.us and john@investec.us; (website) www.investecadvisorygroup.com.

Your Home:
A Roof Over Your Retirement Years

Dennis Haber, JD, CSA
Senior Funding Group

An incredible growth is occurring in the senior marketplace—the 85 and over age range. According to the latest census,[1] 58,000 people reached 100 years of age. Because seniors are living longer, they have a higher probability of requiring long term care. For example, 10 percent of seniors who reach age 65 will suffer from Alzheimer's Disease, while 47 percent over 85 will suffer from the same malady.[2] Alzheimer's will become a 21st Century epidemic as it begins its assault on the baby boomers.

Most importantly, many seniors are under-insured and ill-prepared for the expenses associated with long term healthcare. According to Health Insurance Association of America study (2000), 84 percent of seniors that have not purchased long-term care insurance cite cost as a reason. Why? Because they can't afford it.

As people live longer their money must last longer as well. With the spate of bad and/or low return on their investments, rising property taxes, and poor financial planning, seniors on all economic levels are having a difficult time. The question becomes, "How can seniors get more money into their pockets quickly?"

What's a Retiree to Do?

The financial and emotional toll of aging can wreak havoc within the family unit. The adult children who have children of their own may have the

---

[1] U.S. Census Bureau International Data Base,2000
[2] Alzheimer's Association (1996)

added financial—and sometimes physical—burden of meeting the needs of their parents. They are forced to become caregivers because the parent's funds are scarce. About 20 percent of family caregivers spend 40 hours per week caring for their loved ones.[3] Sometimes children will sacrifice promotions at work, or may have to quit a job to take care of mom and/or dad. It is not unusual for a child to suffer from burnout soon after taking on this responsibility. If another sibling is not available to lend a hand or respite care is not affordable, then the impending situation is a recipe for disaster. It is estimated that some of the "sandwich generation" will spend more time providing elder care than childcare. The important question is: can a parent regain his or her independence and release their children to live their own lives?

Today, many seniors are literally sitting on a gold mine estimated at $2 trillion in assets that represent over $950 billion that can be converted into cash.

Yes. And the solution is literally right above their heads. Today, many seniors are literally sitting on a gold mine estimated at $2 trillion in assets that represent over $950 billion that can be converted into cash.

The gold mine? Their homes.

This sleeping revenue can provide the solution to many seniors' economic crisis. However, while some options are commonly known and implemented, they may not always be the best choices. For example:

Choice #1: A senior can sell his or her home.

REASONS WHY THIS CHOICE MAY NOT WORK: Statistics show that seniors do not want to move. Their goal is to stay in the environment that contains so much of their personal and family history. They want to live in an area that is familiar. Their doctors, friends and family are close by. Often the house is the center of the story of their life.

After the home is sold, the senior has to find a new place to live. Very often a new smaller home will cost more than the home they just sold. Many times, they do not have the money for the down payment or the funds to cover the closing costs. Even if a senior could move, often the emotional toll is devastating. A sale becomes financially impractical. Renting new quarters also creates anxiety because the senior is also forced to give up the place that stores so many of their memories. When renting, they are

---

[3] 2002 Edition Society of Certified Senior Advisor, p 178

subject to rules and regulations of the apartment complex. When considering these choices, the undercurrent of thought remains that they prefer to stay in their current home.

Choice #2: A senior can get a traditional loan.

REASONS WHY THIS CHOICE MAY NOT WORK: Typically when one applies for a mortgage, income, assets and credit are reviewed. (Front-end and back-end ratios are determined. This means that the debt-to-income ratio cannot exceed predetermined numbers based upon the particular loan program). Credit scores are carefully perused. While some seniors may qualify for a traditional loan, they do not want the "headache" or the responsibility of paying it back. Making those monthly payments is something they can do without.

Many seniors, on the other hand, cannot qualify for a traditional mortgage. They do not have the income and/or the assets and/or the credit to be approved.

The Reverse Mortgage to the Rescue

Most people are familiar with a forward mortgage which is the traditional

---

More About the Reverse Mortgage

As of this writing, the term "reverse mortgage" generally refers to any one of three distinct reverse mortgage programs that are utilized nationally. By far, the most popular is the Federal Housing Administration's HECM (Home Equity Conversion Mortgage).[4] This program accounts for greater than 90 percent[5] of all reverse mortgage loans obtained. The steady increase in closed reverse mortgage (HECM) loans has caused Congress to increase the number of reverse mortgages the government can insure. The passage of additional legislation will permit HUD (Housing and Urban Development) to insure an unlimited number of such loans.[6] This would mean that the reverse mortgage program is here to stay. In effect, it is finally being recognized as the important financial instrument that it is.

The shifting demographics in this country require that this program remain strong and viable. It also requires that Congress give HUD the ability to insure this program into the future without regard to a predetermined cap. That is why it is important for the Senate (the House of Representatives has already passed The Reverse Mortgage To Help America's Seniors Act) to also pass this legislation without delay.

The last census suggests the following: In 2000 there were 35 million seniors 65 and older. This number will grow to 70 million over the next 20 years. In 2000 there were 4 million seniors reaching their 85th birthday. It is estimated that in the year 2050 this country will have 20 million seniors 85 and older. ◆

---

[4] There has been a 500% growth in origination volume between 2001 and 2004 NRMLA Press Release February 21, 2005

[5] National Reverse Mortgage Lenders Association News Release November 10, 2005. Revised in December 15th Press Release 2005.

[6] HUD is authorized to insure 150,000 reverse mortgages 12USC § 1715z20(g). The number of HECM reverse mortgages has steadily increased. This figure is now approaching 100,000. Reverse Mortgage Advisor Volume 8.1, Winter 2005. The above section was amended to allow 250,000 units to be insured. The Reverse Mortgage to Help America's Seniors Act passed the House Of Representatives in December 2005 (H.R.2892) and is still awaiting approval in the Senate (S.1710). This legislation finally removes all caps on reverse mortgage loans that HUD can insure.

mortgage loan where monthly payments are made to a bank. As those payments are made, the unpaid principal balance decreases (amortizes), while the equity in the home continues to grow. This kind of loan is commonplace. However, fewer people are familiar with a reverse mortgage, a loan in which the opposite occurs. No monthly mortgage payments are made by the senior borrower. In fact, the bank pays the borrower each month (if the borrower chooses this type of payment). These two things cause the unpaid balance to continue to grow. Accordingly, the equity in the home decreases. This kind of loan is quite remarkable as it transforms value and equity into usable cash. As a result, it allows seniors to fulfill their unrealized dreams. After all, the equity they have in their home is often the largest untapped asset many seniors have.

A reverse mortgage affords [seniors] the opportunity to remain in the home they love.

The good news is that reverse mortgage approval is not based upon a showing of specific income, asset, nor typical credit worthiness.[7] To ensure that a closing can take place, all unsatisfied judgments and liens must be paid at or before closing and the borrower must show that any Chapter 7 bankruptcy has been discharged. In essence, when one chooses a reverse mortgage, a non-performing, "dead" asset is transposed into a performing, "live" asset. The senior can unlock the equity in the home that is just sitting there doing nothing. Before a reverse mortgage was on a senior's radar scope, those who couldn't qualify for a loan could only realize the significant equity by the sale of the home. A reverse mortgage affords them the opportunity to remain in the home that they love.

Let us look more closely at why selling the home and obtaining a traditional mortgage are not acceptable choices for an overwhelming majority of senior citizens.

Why Is It So Great?

A reverse mortgage works because a senior receives a sum of money from a bank without having to make those dreaded monthly payments.[8] As long as the home is used as a primary residence,[9] the property taxes are paid,[10] the homeowner's insurance is paid,[11] and the property is kept

---

[7] Any delinquent Federal Debt must be brought current or paid before HUD will let a senior be eligible for the HECM program. HUD Handbook 4235.1 Revision No. 1 paragraphs 4-3(A,B, and C)

[8] 24 CFR § 206.27(8)

[9] 24 CFR § 206.27(2)(i), 24 CFR § 206.27(2)(ii),24 CFR §206.3 and 24 CFR §206.39

[10] 24 CFR § 206.27(6)

[11] 24 CFR § 206.27(6)

in good repair,[12] the loan does not have to be repaid. When the last (spouse) homeowner passes away,[13] or does not use the property as their primary residence,[14] then the loan will be repaid. At this time, the home is put on the market. Notice the difference. The home is sold by the senior or their estate when the senior no longer has a use for the home.

A reverse mortgage has the pliability and flexibility to meet many needs of the senior borrower. For example, the HECM program permits title in a trust,[15] retained life estate,[16] or leasehold interest.[17]

The tax-free proceeds[18] can provide enough money to purchase a long term care policy, or other insurance. The funds can act as an emergency investment vehicle, estate planning device, or a retirement facilitator.

Your Children's Inheritance

The one issue that gives a senior pause is the personal issue of inheritance. Some seniors feel an obligation to leave their home "mortgage free" to their children. Some children will insist that their parents refrain from obtaining a reverse mortgage because they want to receive the home free and clear when the parents die.

Co-op Apartments

Clearly, what is missing is allowing HUD to insure a reverse mortgage on a co-op apartment. Currently there is only one program, a proprietary program, that embraces reverse mortgages for a cooperative apartment. HUD needs to explore ways of allowing a program for cooperatives. This proprietary program for co-ops is done only in the State of New York. New York was chosen because the city has a high density of cooperative apartments. This means that Tenant Shareholders of cooperative apartments in other jurisdictions cannot take advantage of the reverse mortgage programs. The good news as of this writing is that HUD is considering the use of the HECM program for co-ops. This will impact all 50 states.

On the other hand, many children would also rather see their parents live a life of independence and dignity. They encourage their parents to obtain a reverse mortgage. In fact, a reverse mortgage is a life saver for the senior as well as the children. When the parent gets a reverse mortgage, the children do not have to provide monetary aid to their parents. It alleviates the burden the children feel, as they usually have children of their own. In addition, they may be contributing to a college fund for their kid's education, or a retirement fund for themselves. They are strapped. Many really are not in a position to help their parents. Therefore, a reverse mortgage often turns out to be a real life saver for both sets of families.

---

[12] 24 CFR § 206.27(5)

[13] 24 CFR § 206.27(c)

[14] 24 CFR §206.27(2)(i)

[15] Mortgagee Letter 93-22

[16] 24 CFR § 206.27(c)

[17] 24 CFR § 206.27(c)

[18] Proceeds from a loan are not considered income.

Equity Into Cash

The amount of money a borrower can receive depends upon the age of the youngest borrower, the value of the home up to the maximum claim amount[19] and the current expected interest rate.[20] The minimum age requirement to obtain a reverse mortgage is 62.[21] The age of the youngest borrower is used when there are two borrowers.[22] It is important to remember that older borrowers can convert more of the value/equity into cash. For example, assuming the same housing value, in the same community, a 75-year-old can extract more equity than a 65-year-old borrower.

The tax-free proceeds from a reverse mortgage can be received in a variety of ways. The borrower can choose a lump sum payment or monthly payments for as long as they live in the home or monthly payments for a term of years, or a line of credit.[23] These options can even be combined, The absolutely remarkable thing about the tenure payments is that the payments will last as long as the home is used as the principal residence. This means that the payments will continue even if no equity is left in the home and even if the total payments received exceed the original principal limit. The tenure payments will continue even if the amount received exceeds the amount noted in the security instrument.[24] Unlike other programs, there is no minimum draw (tenure, term or credit line) that a borrower is required to take.[25] They can even switch between payment options.[26] Again, a reverse mortgage is very flexible. It is like a straw that can be bent, twisted and molded to fit borrowers' changing needs.

Remember, a fundamental purpose of the reverse mortgage is to allow seniors to dream again of a better life for themselves and for their family.

The borrower has sole and total discretion when it comes to using the proceeds. Accordingly, seniors have used the proceeds to make needed home repairs, pay off credit card debt, judgments, mortgages and tax

---

[19] 24 CFR § 206.3 The Maximum Claim Amount is the lesser of the appraised value or FHA lending limit for a single family home in a particular county. The highest FHA lending limit is currently $362,790. This means that if one owns a home that has a value of $500,000 The FHA will count $362,790 of the $500,000 value in determining how much can be realized.

[20] HUD Handbook 4235.1-Revision No.1 paragraphs 1-4A(1) 24 CFR § 206.3

[21] 24 CFR § 206.33

[22] 24 CFR § 206.33

[23] 24 CFR § 206.25

[24] 24 CFR §206.19(a)(b)(c) In spite of the language in (f), FHA does not keep track of the amount noted in the security instruments, and therefore will continue to make payments until the term expires, the credit line is depleted or the home is sold in the case of tenure payments.

[25] 24 CFR § 206.25(g)

[26] 24 CFR §206.26(c)

liens. Some have used the proceeds for home healthcare requirements. Others have purchased second homes, or traveled to their favorite places. The money can even be used to provide for a grandchild's college education. Some have even purchased different types of insurance policies. Remember, a fundamental purpose of the reverse mortgage is to allow seniors to dream again of a better life for themselves and for their families. It is important that they realize those dreams while maintaining their independence. A reverse mortgage accomplishes these goals.

An Informed Decision

Although the qualification process is easy, a reverse mortgage applicant must attend or receive reverse mortgage counseling from an approved HUD counseling entity or from the AARP Foundation Network of Counselors before the process can go forward, which now includes counselors from the National Foundation of Credit Counselors and Money Management International.[27] This is a good thing as it provides the seniors with additional information as well as possible alternatives to their situation. It ensures that the seniors are making an informed decision. As a further protective measure, a lender cannot start the actual processing of the loan until the counseling has been completed. This means that such things as appraisal, title and credit report can only be ordered *after* the counseling has been completed and the borrower has confirmed his or her desire to obtain a reverse mortgage. However, the application and disclosures can be signed *prior* to the client receiving the counseling.[28] I believe in getting family members together to discuss the situation. It is important that the entire family understand the benefits of this innovative program.

There are several distinct types of reverse mortgage loan programs. As more investors become comfortable with the program, the "model" FHA/HECM program will change as well. As of 2006, however, the HECM loan comes in just two varieties: The interest rate can adjust only monthly or yearly.

The other loan type is Fannie Mae's Homekeeper loan. This program is more conservative than the HECM, although the FNMA lending limit is now $417,000. The HECM, with a top lending limit of $362,790, will provide greater proceeds for a home located in a county that utilizes this top limit.[29] Remember these limits change every year. Also remember that these limits are just one of the "ingredients" that determine how much one can receive. Age and expected interest rate are the other "ingredients."

[27] 24 CFR §206.41 Mortgagee Letter 2005-44.

[28] Mortgagee Letter 2004-25 However Mortgagee Letter 2006-25 now provides title can be ordered prior to counseling

[29] As of this writing the HUD maximum lending limit for a single family home is $362,790. The significance of living in a home in a county that utilizes the maximum FHA lending limit is this: Take two seniors with identical age, property values and expected interest rates. One senior lives in Jericho NY-Nassau County (FHA limit of $362,790) and one lives in Nashville, TN- Davidson County (FHA limit of $226,100). The individual living in Nassau County will receive more proceeds than the individual living in Davidson County.

As of this year (2006) the HECM lending limits range from a low of $200,160 to a high of $362,790.

The third type of program is the Cash Advantage®. Under this program, a senior can realize even more money from the equity in the home. It generally works best when the home has an appraised value that exceeds $500,000 and the senior is in his or her mid-to-late seventies. Also this program has been used for co-ops, irrevocable trusts (case-by-case basis) and second homes (case-by-case basis).

A HECM[30] and Homekeeper reverse mortgage can only be made against a principal residence. FHA will make a loan against a one to four family unit, approved condo and PUDs.[31] However, single family lending limits are used in two to four unit properties. Fannie Mae will only make loans against one-unit properties, approved condos and PUDs. As mentioned above, a reverse mortgage program recently became available for co-ops, under the Cash Advantage® program. It is hoped that sometime soon, FHA and Fannie Mae will also permit reverse mortgages on co-ops.

Conclusion

Many people think of reverse mortgages simply as a way to help our elders pay their bills. The program, in a relatively short time, has evolved into a very potent economic and financial tool. Government, for example, is looking at reverse mortgages as a way to halt the rising Medicaid costs. The DRA (Deficit Reduction Act) that passed Congress this year specifically makes anyone who owns a home with $500,000 in equity ineligible for Medicaid benefits unless they obtain a home equity loan or a reverse mortgage. (The states have the opportunity to raise the amount to $750,000.)

Government should also be looking at the reverse mortgage loan as a way to recycle "grant" money. Instead of a grant program that provides funds for various purposes, a municipality can provide the funds through their own reverse mortgage program. The funds will be paid back on a *non-recourse basis* when the home is sold. This will enable government to help more people because the money gets recycled with interest. This is better than providing grant money that is eventually forgiven.

The reverse mortgage industry must also do its job. Imagine for a moment if new programs were created that put even more money into the hands of the seniors without increasing the banks' risks. That would be a wonderful thing. Programs that waive the up-front mortgage insurance premium and eliminate the service set-asides would be a good place to start. Also, the industry must expand the options available to accountants and financial planners. Reverse mortgages should be able to fit into a

---

[30] 24 CFR § 206.3
[31] 24 CFR § 206.45; Mortgagee Letter 90-17 (I);Mortgagee Letter 96-15;24 CFR § 206.51;
   12 USC § 1715z-20(d)(3)

financial plan that contains a Qualified Personal Residence Trust and a Charitable Remainder Trust, for example.

The reverse mortgage banks and the government must work together to simplify the process and the paperwork. Imagine again for a moment if it took a week to close a reverse mortgage loan rather than the many weeks it now takes. The underwriting process also needs to be simplified.

The originators must be well trained to deal with the demanding and different needs of our seniors. If all such originators also obtained credentials that taught them about the special legal, social, and medical challenges their clients faced, that would definitely be a good thing.

Our neighborhood banks must stop giving our elders loans that they know cannot be paid back. Banks should be required to provide seniors with a disclosure that informs them that they may be eligible for a reverse mortgage.

Our neighborhood banks must stop giving our elders loans that they know cannot be paid back. Banks should be required to provide seniors with a disclosure that informs them that they may be eligible for a reverse mortgage. Many seniors are put in peril because they have "qualified" for a loan they cannot pay back. Many who need additional funds never knew that there was another option (like a reverse mortgage).

Exciting things will be happening within the financial services industry in the next few years. The momentum and excitement that currently exists will be sustained only if the programs become better, more flexible and if more caring people enter this field. This field is not for those lenders that are simply looking to expand their product line.

The HECM loan is safe.[32] It allows seniors to use the equity in their homes to realize their many dreams. One of these dreams is to remain in their home. Seniors are beginning to understand that age does, in fact, have its privileges. Imagine getting a loan without the requirement of paying the bank each month. Further imagine that this continues for as long as the home is used as a principal residence. Think about all the things a senior can accomplish with a reverse mortgage. All of a sudden,

---

[32] There are safeguards to insure that the senior receives their money from their lender on time. The Secretary of HUD under 24 CFR § 206.121 can investigate the particular complaint, order sanctions against the lender under 24 CFR § 206.201 and under 24 CFR § 206.117 can take action to make sure a mortgagor gets their appropriate payment(s) under such circumstance.

many more people wish they were at least 62, because they, too, do not want the stress of making those monthly mortgage payments and want to dream again.

Because many seniors generally have done a poor job of preparing for retirement, a reverse mortgage will go a long way toward alleviating the stress as well as their money concerns.

◆◆◆

Dennis Haber, Esq, Executive Vice President of Senior Funding Group, is an authority on reverse mortgages. His articles on the topic have been published in various national and local periodicals, including *Senior Market Advisor, Nassau Lawyer, Suffolk Lawyer, New York Mortgage Press, The Cooperator, Real Estate Weekly* and *Elder Law Attorney* a publication of the New York State Bar Association, to name a few. His ground-breaking book *Piggy Bank Your Home For A Brighter Today & Tomorrow* explains reverse mortgage concepts and is revolutionizing how families view reverse mortgages.

He is an attorney and Certified Senior Advisor (CSA) who devotes his time to changing the lives of senior citizens by introducing them to reverse mortgages. In 2005, he submitted testimony to Congress on the "Reverse Mortgages To Help America's Seniors Act" and in 2006 he received from the National Reverse Mortgage Lenders Association an achievement award for exemplary service to the reverse mortgage industry. He was also named to the advisory counsel for the largest reverse mortgage lender in the country.

Dennis is in demand nationally as a speaker on the benefits of reverse mortgages. He addresses mortgage industry groups, bar associations, senior groups, accounting associations and the financial planning industry.

Dennis Haber can be reached at Senior Funding Group, 247 West Old Country Road, Hicksville, NY 11801; (tel) 516.938.6600 x208; (cell) 516.551.2189; (email) denhaber@aol.com.

Still Time to Invest:
Stocks, Bonds, Mutual Funds & Separate Accounts

Michael J. Searcy, President
Searcy Financial Services, Inc.

The world of investing is vast and can be intimidating. With so many options, it is easy to feel overwhelmed. However, we hope to give you the 30,000-foot hover—that is, give you a bird's-eye view of the different types of investment strategies. Then, we will take you down to 10,000 feet to give you a more detailed view of the forest (stocks, bonds, and mutual funds). Finally, we will bring you to the tops of the trees, showing you how to choose different investment types. We will not get into all of the details because there is simply too much information; it would fill an entire forest! However, we will point you in the direction of the places and people who can guide you through the trees at ground level. We believe that this approach will be the best way we can empower you to develop a successful investment plan. At this point, you have a choice: either you will do the research and investing yourself, or you will delegate it to someone else. Either way, you must do your homework and be an informed investor.

Global Fiduciary Standards of Excellence

There are many ways to invest; knowing the basic concepts and vocabulary is key to knowing how your money is being invested and why. This is especially true if you allow someone to help you manage your future. NOTE: If you plan on hiring someone to help you, choose a fiduciary who adheres to the Global Fiduciary Standards of Excellence. These standards were developed by The Foundation for Fiduciary Studies, the only national entity that seeks to define and substantiate specific investment fiduciary practices that are applicable to investment advisors, trustees, and investment committee members. The Foundation for Fiduciary Studies is also the only organization in the country that provides training programs and professional designations based on investment fiduciary standards of care: Accredited Investment Fiduciary™ (AIF®) and Accredited Investment Fiduciary Analyst™ (AIFA®).

A fiduciary is any person who is responsible for managing the assets of another person and stands in a special relationship of trust, confidence and/or legal responsibility. In other words, they must act in your best interest, not simply sell you products that may or may not fit your needs. The Global Fiduciary Standards of Excellence are universally recognized standards that fiduciaries should meet. There are standards for different types of fiduciaries.

- *Investment Stewards:* Includes trustees and investment committee members.
- *Investment Advisors:* Includes financial advisors, broker-consultants, wealth managers, financial consultants and financial planners.
- *Investment Managers:* Includes separate account managers (SAM) and mutual funds.

You can find more information regarding the specific standards associated with these fiduciaries at the Foundation for Fiduciary Studies' website: www.fi360.com

Steps to Your Investment Vision

What is the vision for your future? In other words, what is the purpose for your investments? If you called a bakery to order a birthday cake and did not give them any direction regarding design, icing or flavor, would you be surprised if the cake didn't turn out the way you imagined? Of course not! Likewise, your vision for the future will most likely be different than that of a neighbor, relative or investment advisor. Knowing your desired outcome will guide you in developing a plan that is right for you.

Goals are the first tangible step toward making your vision a reality. They should be measurable and point directly back to your vision.

Goals are the first tangible step toward making your vision a reality. They should be measurable and point directly back to your vision. To stay on track, you may need to periodically revisit and reevaluate your goals. You may find that 10 years down the road you want different things out of life. If this were the case, your goals, and perhaps your plan, would need to be adjusted accordingly.

Next, you need to develop a timeline for achieving your vision. When do you want to begin drawing on funds to live out your vision? For example, if your objective is retirement in 15 years at age 65, then your investment design must encompass the time you expect to enjoy *after* you retire (at least another 25-30 years). You will want to keep your money working for you throughout the entire period, even while you are drawing on your nest egg.

After you have defined your vision and corresponding goals, you need to develop a plan. Most people limit their investment success because they do not follow a plan. They have no direction; they do not follow a disciplined process. Using the recipe analogy, how can you expect to get the kind of cake you want if you are throwing everything from your pantry into the mixing bowl? Just as you need a *chocolate* cake recipe in order to bake a *chocolate* cake, you need to choose an appropriate investment plan that will result in achieving your vision.

Start by asking yourself, "What is my personal level of risk?" This should be determined by your own level of comfort; if you are going to lose sleep at night because you are worrying about the status of your investments, you might want to choose a more conservative, less risky approach. What good is it for you to achieve your vision if you are miserable throughout the journey? You should be comfortable with how your money is working for you. To assess your "personal risk level," complete the quiz on page 36.

The proper definition of risk as it relates to investing is a much-debated one. The definition usually depends on the financial practitioner you are speaking with and his or her specific background and training. We believe the more encompassing definition of risk, as it relates to our clients, is *the possibility of financial harm*. Other factors to consider are inflation and your time horizon; the shorter the time horizon, the less time you have to recover from a downturn in the market. Thus, if you have more time to invest you can afford to invest in "riskier" investments. However, the level of risk with which you are personally comfortable should dictate the final plan design and investment selections.

Now that you have decided your risk level, you can choose a plan that will guide your investment decisions (or the decisions of the person to whom you have delegated). There are two ways to invest: you can either own or loan. When you invest in stocks, stock mutual funds or with separate account managers (SAM) who focus on stocks, you essentially own a piece of the underlying companies represented. This type of investing is called "equity" and the potential for appreciation is higher, but there

What Kind of Investor Am I?

Rate the following statements on a scale of 1 to 4, with 1 being most true and 4 being least true. (Circle your response.)

1. I like predictability and routine in my life.	1	2	3	4
2. I would rather work longer than reduce my standard of living in retirement.	1	2	3	4
3. I don't like surprises.	1	2	3	4
4. I am not optimistic about my financial future.	1	2	3	4
5. I am more concerned about protecting my assets than about growth.	1	2	3	4
6. I do not make investment decisions comfortably or easily.	1	2	3	4
7. It is more important that I receive a good return in any one year than for my long-term returns to out-perform inflation.	1	2	3	4
8. When do I expect to need most of the money from my investment portfolio?	1 less than 6 years	2 7-9 years	3 10-14 years	4 15+ years
9. If I took a significant loss in a particular investment, how easily could I adapt to the situation?	1 not well	2 reasonably well	3 well	4 very well
10. If a particular investment dropped in value by 20% in less than one year, which of the following would be my response?	1 can't sleep at night	2 fret about it	3 continue to monitor it	4 invest more

If you most frequently circled: 1 = Conservative Investor, 2 = Moderate Investor, 3= Moderately Aggressive Investor, 4= Aggressive Investor is more risk involved. When you invest in bonds, bond mutual funds, mortgages, Certificates of Deposit (CDs), or money market accounts, you are loaning your money to be used by another entity. This type of investing is considered "fixed income and cash equivalents" and there is less appreciation, but also less risk involved. Generally speaking, the more money you have in equities, the more risk you take, but the potential for growth is greater. Conversely, the more money you have in fixed income and cash equivalents, the less risk you take, but the potential for growth is also lower.

"Asset allocation" is the process of dividing a portfolio among equities, fixed income and cash equivalents. Just as a recipe tells you how much of each ingredient you should put into the bowl, the asset allocation tells you where to invest your money, reducing risk because it diversifies the portfolio. Diversification is a key component of your asset allocation. In fact, poor diversification can be disastrous for achieving your vision. During the 1990s the world of technology was booming. Tech stocks were hot; returns were astronomical. Investors who had previously allocated 10% of their portfolios to technology found themselves tempted to invest more and more to get a bigger piece of the action. Many investors allocated the bulk of their portfolio into technology stocks, rather than spreading their funds over a wide range of investments. In 2000, the bottom fell out and tech stock prices plummeted, as did the value of many investors' portfolios. This is a painful example of not maintaining a prudent portfolio diversification. Had their portfolios been more diversified, the results of this crash would not have been so catastrophic for so many investors.

There are many different ways to allocate between "owning" and "loaning." Here are just a few different examples of asset allocations:

Aggressive: Younger investors typically use this plan; a good example of this would be 95% of funds invested in equities, 5% of funds invested in fixed income or cash equivalents.

Moderately Aggressive: This plan is still considered somewhat aggressive with a 10+ year time horizon; a good example of this would be 80% of funds invested in equities, 20% of funds invested in fixed income and cash equivalents.

Moderate: Investors who are retired or approaching retirement typically use this plan; a good example of this would be 60% of funds invested in equities, 40% of funds invested in fixed income and cash equivalents.

Conservative: This plan is ideal for someone who has excess funds that produce adequate income, even at a lower total return; a good example of this would be 40% of funds invested in equities, 60% of funds invested in fixed income and cash equivalents.

Let your vision (the kind of cake you want) help you select the right asset allocation plan (the right recipe). Your plan will help you make decisions in the face of multiple options. When you see everyone jumping on a bandwagon, you can determine its suitability by comparing it to your plan. It is very tempting to invest in something because a relative, co-worker or even news media are talking about it; it is in our very nature to follow the crowd! We rely on and respect the opinions of those in our lives, so why not join in? Remember, their vision and goals are probably quite different from yours. So, you must make decisions based on what will help you reach your vision. Resist the temptation!

Choosing Your Investment Ingredients

Now that you have chosen a plan (i.e. recipe), you need to choose the investments (ingredients.) If you go to the grocery store to buy a bag of flour, you will quickly notice there are many brands and types of flour. How do you know which one to buy? Choosing investments pose a similar dilemma because there are so many options. Although there are a multitude of hybrid investment products containing the blended elements of both fixed income and equity, due to the space constraints of this chapter we will not elaborate on them here. Instead, we will first focus on fixed income "ingredients," and then we will turn our attention to equity. The most common categories of "fixed income and cash equivalents" are:

Bonds: Essentially an "IOU" with which the investor loans money to an entity (company or government) that borrows the funds for a specific time period and interest rate.

Commercial Mortgage-Backed Security: A bond or other financial obligation secured by a pool of mortgage loans. Also known as "Fannie Maes and Ginnie Maes."

Certificate of Deposit (CD): A savings certificate, usually by a commercial bank, entitling the bearer to receive interest. CDs have a maturity date (generally ranging from one month to five years), fixed interest rate and can be issued at any denomination.

Money Market: Deals in short-term debt and other liquid monetary instruments.

The most common categories of equities are:

Stocks: Basic investment tool that allows investors to buy an interest in an enterprise owned and run by others. Stocks are classified as small cap, mid cap, or large cap.

Small Cap: Smaller companies, whose market capitalization is between approximately $300 million and $2 billion.

Mid Cap: Medium-sized companies, having a market capitalization between approximately $2 billion and $10 billion.

Large Cap: Large companies, having a market capitalization between approximately $10 billion and $200 billion.

Privately Owned Real Estate: Real estate that you own (i.e. rental house, apartment building, strip shopping center or a commercial building), in which you or your partners are actively involved.

Private Business Ownership: Owning and operating (passively or actively) your own business, which is not publicly owned or traded.

Mutual funds or separately managed accounts are not a category of equity or fixed income. Instead, it is merely the way you select to manage the equities within your portfolio through the use of a professional money manager. Mutual funds are a diversified way of having a professional manager buy a variety of stocks and manage them for you. (Note: They can be a mix of stocks *and* bonds.) Separately managed accounts are much like mutual funds, except the account is in your name and managed for your benefit alone.

How to Choose a Mutual Fund

Even though you may be familiar with these investments, how do you go about choosing a particular mutual fund? Many people invest in mutual funds or separately managed accounts (SMAs) because they diversify the portfolio (due to the variety and number of stocks and bonds in which they invest), while providing professional management. We suggest the following steps, created by Fiduciary*360*, as *bare minimum* in screening mutual funds and separate account managers.[1] If a mutual fund does not meet one or more of these screens, it does not necessarily mean you should eliminate it. However, you may want to do additional research before proceeding. You will notice that this process relies heavily on peer group comparison. This sounds easy enough; however, it can be difficult to determine the appropriate peer group because they are sometimes classified differently across databases. For example: Standard & Poor's may classify a mutual fund as a "Large Cap Value," but Morningstar may classify that same fund as "Large Cap Growth." (You can find most classifications through any Internet fund search.) Although this outlines the steps for mutual funds, you would use the same minimum standards when evaluating a separate account manager.

1. Confirm that it is a regulated mutual fund.

2. Check to see if the mutual fund is consistently categorized within the same style and peer group.

3. Compare the mutual fund's performance to those in its peer group,

---

[1] Fiduciary*360*, *Prudent Practices for Investment Advisors* (Sewickley, PA: Fiduciary*360*, 2006).

that is, those mutual funds that are similar in nature for the one-, three-, and five-year cumulative periods. It should meet the median or better.

4. Compare the mutual fund's alpha and/or Sharpe ratio, which are published risk-adjusted performance statistical measurements, with its peer group's median.

5. Find out when the mutual fund was created. The suggested *minimum* age is three years.

6. Determine the total assets within a mutual fund. The minimum threshold is $75 million.

7. Make sure the mutual fund's holdings are consistent with style. For example, a large cap mutual fund should not hold more than 20% in cash, fixed income, or any other unrelated asset class.

8. Compare the mutual fund's expense ratio/fees to those in its asset class. The fees should not be in the bottom (most expensive) quartile.

9. Look for high turnover/organization problems within the mutual fund's management team. The team should be in place for at least two years.

Note: Many firms maintain their own proprietary standards that far exceed these, and you may develop your own as well, based on your education, training and experience. The above represent the bare minimum standards that you should consider when choosing a mutual fund or SAM.

How to Choose Stocks

There are many theories and ideas among experts about how to choose stocks. There are basically two types of investors: active and passive investors. Active investors attempt to "beat" the market,[2] as measured by a particular index,[3] while passive investors do not make decisions about what to invest in; they simply copy an index.

Once you have decided what kind of investor you are, there are many philosophies that may guide your investment decisions.

Bottom-up analysis: Investing strategy that focuses on the fundamentals of individual stocks, as opposed to the state of the overall economy.

Top-down analysis: Analysis that begins with a look at the overall economic picture, narrowing it down to sectors, industries and companies that are expected to perform well. Analysis of the fundamentals of a given stock is typically the final step.

Fundamental analysis: A method where an investor seeks to fully re-

---

[2] When you hear about "the market," you are hearing about a place (such as the New York Stock Exchange) where stocks in publicly traded companies are primarily bought and sold.

[3] An index is a statistical measure of change in the market, essentially an imaginary portfolio of stocks representing the market or a segment of it.

search a company in order to determine its intrinsic value as compared to the price currently listed on the stock market.[4]

Technical analysis: Analysis in which investors use stock price data to look for price trends and patterns affecting a stock's price movement and then make buy/sell decisions based on those factors.[5]

When you have decided what type of investor you will be and what underlying philosophy (or methodology) you will utilize, you can choose a stock selection approach.

Market timing approach: Market timers attempt to predict when the market, or specific stocks, will rise and fall.[6]

Contrarian approach: This approach typically bets against recent happenings in the market in the hope of making a profit. For example, buying out-of-favor stocks and selling them when they're popular again.[7]

Income approach: Income investors focus on securing a steady income stream, investing in companies with consistently high dividend payments instead of worrying about capital gains.[8]

Growth approach: In this approach, investors typically focus on the potential for a company to grow its earnings over time by investing in companies with high earnings growth.[9]

Value approach: This approach invests in stocks that are selling at attractive prices (or bargains) relative to what the investor estimates as the company's intrinsic value.[10]

Growth at a Reasonable Price approach (GARP): With this approach, investors look for companies that have the potential to grow their earnings, but resist paying high prices to attain that growth.[11]

Growth and quality approach: A hybrid approach in which the investor is not searching for questionable companies at bargain prices or exceptional companies at outrageous prices, but good companies at good prices.[12]

Dogs of the Dow approach: A stock selection strategy in which investors purchase the most out of favor stocks in the Dow Jones Industrial

---

[4] Benjamin Graham and David L. Dodd, *Security Analysis* (United States of America: McGraw-Hill Company, Inc., 1951).

[5] Deborah Weir, *Timing the Market: How to Profit in the Stock Market Using the Yield Curve, Technical Analysis, and Cultural Indicators* (Hoboken, New Jersey: John Wiley & Sons, 2006).

[6] IBID

[7] David Dreman, *Contrarian Investment Strategies in the Next Generation* (New York: Simon & Schuster, 1998).

[8] Lowell Miller, *The Single Best Investment: Consistently Creating Wealth with Dividend Growth* (Chicago: Independent Publishers Group, 2006).

[9] Phillip A. Fisher and Kenneth L. Fisher, *Common Stocks and Uncommon Profits and Other Writings* (Hoboken, New Jersey: John Wiley & Sons, Inc., 2003).

[10] Bruce C. N. Greenwald et al., *Value Investing: From Graham to Buffett and Beyond* (Hoboken, New Jersey: John Wiley & Sons, Inc., 2001).

[11] Thomas P. Au, *A Modern Approach to Graham and Dodd Investing* (Hoboken, New Jersey: John Wiley & Sons, Inc., 2004).

[12] Robert G. Hagstrom, *The Warren Buffet Way* (Hoboken, New Jersey: John Wiley & Sons, Inc., 2004).

Index, hoping they will go from "bad" to "less bad."[13]

CANSLIM approach: This approach requires an analysis of Current Earnings, Annual Earnings, New Things, Shares Outstanding, Leading Stocks, Institutional Ownership and Market Conditions to determine if a stock is appropriate for addition to a portfolio.[14]

Insider Activity approach: This stock purchase approach watches what insiders at a company are doing with their stock, assuming the people at the top have inside knowledge.[15]

Sector Rotation approach: This approach attempts to profit through timing a particular economic cycle, based on the belief that not all sectors of the economy perform well at the same time.[16]

Charting approach: This investment approach is rooted in technical analysis, identifying patterns in stock prices to potentially predict the future movement of stocks.[17]

Relative Strength approach: This approach selects stocks based on its price trend relative to an appropriate index for the same time period.[18]

Short Selling approach: This approach attempts to profit from the anticipated drop in a stock price, hoping to repurchase stock at a lower price than when it was sold.[19]

There are also many theories and practices regarding the management of your investment selection. These include, but are not limited to, the following:

Buy-and-Hold approach: This approach to investing assumes that in the long run, stock prices will rise and ignore any short-term market fluctuations.[20]

Dollar Cost Averaging approach: Investing approach that involves regular ongoing contributions regardless of market volatility, preventing short-term emotion-based decisions on the part of the investor.[21]

Constant Ratio approach: Approach where the same percentage of funds is divided among different assets. When the asset balance is out

[13] Charles B. Carlson, *Winning with the Dow's Losers* (New York: HarperCollins Publishers, Inc., 2004).

[14] William J. O'Neil, *The Successful Investor: What 80 Million People Need to Know to Invest Profitably and Avoid Big Losses* (New York: The McGraw-Hill Companies, 2004).

[15] George Muzea, *The Vital Few vs. the Trivial Many: Invest with the Insiders, Not the Masses* (Hoboken, New Jersey: John Wiley & Sons, Inc., 2005).

[16] Chris Stone, "Sector Rotation: The Essentials." *Investopedia.com*. 3 Feb. 2005. Investopedia, Inc. 25 July 2006 < http://www.investopedia.com/articles/trading/05/020305.asp>.

[17] Robert R. Prechter, Jr., A. J. Frost, and Charles J. Collins, *Elliot Wave Principle: Key to Market Behavior* (Hoboken, New Jersey: John Wiley & Sons, Inc., 2001).

[18] William J. O'Neil, The Successful Investor: What 80 Million People Need to Know to Invest Profitably and Avoid Big Losses (New York: The McGraw-Hill Companies, 2004).

[19] William J. O'Neil, How to Make Money Selling Stocks Short (Hoboken, New Jersey: John Wiley & Sons, Inc., 2005).

[20] Peter Lynch and John Rothchild, One Up on Wall Street: How to Use What You Already Know to Make Money in the Market (New York: Fireside, 1989).

[21] Robert J. Altra, Ph.D. and Thomas L. Mann, Ph.D, "Dollar-Cost Averaging and Seasonality: Some International Evidence."

of line, moving money from outperforming assets to underperforming ones periodically restores it. This system prevents one asset class from dominating the portfolio.

Variable Ratio approach: This strategy is a subset of the constant ratio system and relies on market timing to shift the proportions of the various asset classes contained in the portfolio. Buying low and selling high is built into this strategy, but (like the constant dollar system) prolonged movements in a given direction may harm returns.

The January Effect approach: A stock selection strategy that seeks to buy stocks in the month of January due to market rallies, occurring because of investors buying stocks that have dropped in price following a sell-off at the end of December.[22]

Preserving Gains and Limiting Losses approach: This approach tries to set stop/loss limits on stock positions to trigger at prices that will protect profits and limit losses.[23]

It's Your Vision

Picking your own stock investments and managing a portfolio of stock investments is certainly challenging, but can be a potentially rewarding experience. While we have laid out the basics as to the types of investors, philosophies and approaches most commonly subscribed to, we highly recommend additional reading on each. All of the approaches have had their "day in the sun" at some point in time; however, as you will find while conducting your homework, some have proven more effective than others over the long term.

If you decide that selecting stocks and actively managing your portfolio is for you, we stress that you remember one last thing. Stock investment holdings in your portfolio are not just pieces of paper like lottery tickets, but ownership interests in real businesses. Stock investments have proven over long periods of time to deliver superior returns versus bonds or cash, even though they are more risky. This is due to the fact that over long periods of time, equities reflect the profit growth of real businesses. In fact, some companies return monies back to shareholders in the form of a dividend. This dividend represents a real return to shareholders from the profits earned by the company. You must understand the fundamental basis of why a fractional ownership of a publicly traded company (i.e. a stock) is worth anything at all. In order to enjoy the long-term benefits of participating in the profit growth of a business, investors must look beyond short-term volatility and focus on the likelihood that a certain business will be more valuable in the future than it is today.

---

[22] Robert A. Haugen and Josef Lakonishok, *The Incredible January Effect: The Stock Market's Unsolved Mystery* (Howewood, Illinois: Dow Jones-Irwin, 1987).

[23] "Stop Orders" U.S. Securities and Exchange Commission Fast Answers-Key Topics. 31 May 2002. United States Securities and Exchange Commission. 7 July 2006 http://www.sec.gov/answers/stopord.htm.

There is no such thing as a free lunch, and you will have to do your homework, especially if you decide to manage your investments yourself. If you choose to delegate to someone else, make sure that you are an informed delegator so that you will be able to hold them accountable to manage your portfolio to best accomplish *your* dream. If you have an investment advisor working with you, they are going to have an enormous influence in what you apply to your portfolio and how it is managed. Make it a point to ask them what they believe, why they believe it and what process they use. If they can't discuss it with you on an intelligent and *understandable* basis, they might not be a good fit. In addition, if they do not view themselves as a fiduciary, they may not have your best interests in mind when making investment decisions. Use the Global Fiduciary Standards of Excellence as a guide to help ensure that you are receiving the very best ethical and responsible financial care. Remember, this is your vision (your cake), and you must have a plan (follow a recipe)!

Michael J. Searcy, ChFC, CFP®, AIF®, AIFA® is an Accredited Investment Fiduciary Analyst™ and President of Searcy Financial Services, Inc., an independent, financial planning, wealth management and registered investment advisory firm. Over the past 30-plus years, Michael has been privileged to help a variety of people achieve their vision of an ideal life. His objective is to help his clients focus on accomplishing those things that really matter most to them in their lives. He endeavors to deliver the most accurate and timely information available, while providing the highest quality of products and services through companies and individuals who share his level of commitment to integrity.

Searcy Financial Services, Inc. provides services collectively known as the Comprehensive Financial Planning Process. This analysis includes investment management, retirement planning, insurance analysis and estate planning. Searcy Financial Services, Inc. was included as one of the "Top Wealth Managers" in the nation by *Bloomberg Wealth Manager* magazine in publication years 2001 through 2005 and again in their most recent listing in 2006. Michael can be reached at: Searcy Financial Services, Inc., 13220 Metcalf Ave, Suite 360, Overland Park, KS 66213; (tel) 913.814.3800; (email) mike@searcyfinancial.com.

Michael would like to thank his staff, especially Jessica Maldonado, John Owen, Jr., and Kristin Fillingham, for their contributions to the creation and development of this chapter.

Your 401(k) Rollover And Your IRA

5.

Mike Piershale, Registered Principal
Raymond James Financial Services, Inc.

At the beginning of the 20th century, the average American's life expectancy was less than 50 years. As a result, most people never retired. Today, people are living longer and healthier lives and retirement often lasts 20 years or more. But not surprising, according to surveys from the American Association of Retired Persons (AARP), more than two-thirds of 50- to 70-year-old workers say they plan to work into their retirement years or never retire at all.

Maybe they really enjoy the rewards of working. Or maybe they have no choice but to continue working. For example, here is an eye-opening statistic: If a couple wants an annual retirement income of $85,000 and intends to stop working at age 65, they'll need about $838,000 in savings in order to supplement their Social Security income for 20 years, assuming a seven percent rate of return and four percent inflation rate. If working longer and spending less during your retirement years doesn't appeal to you, you should craft a solid plan ahead of time and think about exactly what retirement means to you.

What Does Retirement Mean to You?

Does it mean you no longer have to spend more than half your time at your job, or running your business? Does it mean the financial freedom to travel, spend more time with the grandkids, or is it simply the luxury of sleeping past the 7 a.m. alarm? Hopefully, it's the financial freedom to do whatever you want to do after your working years. No matter what retirement means to you, it possibly can possibly be the "ultimate vacation" if you take the proper planning steps.

One of the crucial steps to planing your retirement is knowing where your income will come from, and that it will last. The three major sources of retirement income usually fit into these three groups:

1. Government-sponsored programs (Social Security, etc.)

2. Employer-sponsored programs (401(k), 403(b), pension, etc)

3. Personal savings and investments (IRA, Roth IRA, etc.)

Government-Sponsored Programs

Currently, more than 47 million Americans collect some sort of Social Security retirement, disability, or death benefit. Social Security is a pay-as-you-go system, with today's current workers paying the benefits for today's retiree.[1] According to the Social Security Administration (SSA), in 1950 there were 16 workers per beneficiary; today there are three workers per beneficiary, and within 40 years there will be just two workers per beneficiary. The question is: Will Social Security be able to financially support this group?

The latest report from the Social Security trustees claims that by the year 2017 the system will not be taking in enough payroll taxes to pay all benefits promised and will need to tap other resources that make up its fund. They also claim that the Social Security trust fund will be completely exhausted by 2041.[2] This is an alarming statistic, but even if Social Security could support you over the next few years, would you be able to live on a national Social Security average benefit of about $12,000 a year?[3]

Clearly, the answer is "no" for the vast majority of the population. So, the most logical sources to look to for your retirement planning are your employer-sponsored or personal retirement plans (as noted above). Even so, these retirement plans have choices that also raise thought-provoking questions. For example:

1. Which plan will give you the most potential income at retirement?

2. What has the best tax advantages?

3. Will your contribution be deductible?

4. How do you make withdrawals from your plan?

5. How are your withdrawals taxed?

6. Which plan is best for your situation?

7. Can you contribute to more than one retirement plan?

---

[1] ©2006 Forefield, Inc., Used with Permission. All Rights Reserved
[2] Social Security Administration, 2005
[3] IBID

8. How much do you need to contribute?

9. How much does your employer contribute?

We'll review possible answers to these questions and more as we discuss the various types of plans and how they work. But, before we do, here's an overview of why a retirement account may be more appropriate for you than a savings/taxable account. Consider the following:

Most company plans allow for payroll deductions, making it easier for you to budget your money. Plus, contributing to your plan with "before-tax" dollars may help reduce your current taxable income and possibly lower your tax bracket. (Also an additional tax credit may apply for contributions made to certain retirement programs.) Consult your tax advisor for more information. These plans also grow "income tax-deferred" until funds are withdrawn, which is an additional tax benefit. Keep in mind that withdrawals from a tax-deferred retirement plan account before age 59½ may be subject to ordinary income tax and a 10% penalty. Another advantage of an employer retirement plan is the matching contribution many companies will make. Matching contributions can assist in decreasing the cost of saving for retirement. Example: Your employer matches 50 cents on the dollar for the first $4,000 of contributions. If you invest $4,000, your employer provides a $2,000 matching contribution giving you a total of $6,000 based on a $4,000 investment. (To receive the employer match, you normally have to be employed by the company for a certain length of time. This is called, "being vested.")

Of course you'll have to pay tax on the $6,000 (and any earnings) once you start taking withdrawals from the employer plan at retirement. Withdrawals prior to retirement age may be subject to penalties, which will be further discussed later in the chapter. But it's hard to beat the advantages of receiving an employer match because of the leverage demonstrated in the example. There may be some situations where you shouldn't necessarily follow this strategy. For example, you may have reason to believe your employment will terminate before the employer match will become vested, so that you'll forfeit the matching contribution. Or the match may be very small (say, 10 cents on the dollar) while other aspects of the employer plan, like poor investment options, make it very unattractive. In general though, it's a good rule of thumb to look to the employer plan first when matching contributions are available.[4]

Now, let's take a more indepth look at both the personal retirement plans and the employer-sponsored retirement plans.

Personal Retirement Plans – IRAs

What is an Individual Retirement Account (IRA)? It's an account that provides federal income tax benefits for retirement investments. It is NOT

---

4 Tax Guide For Investors www.fairmark.com.

an investment itself. Specifically, with an IRA you can set aside earned income up to a specified amount each year and may be able to deduct the contributions from taxable income, if qualified, with the contributions and interest being tax-deferred until retirement. There are two types: the traditional IRA and the Roth IRA.

What are the contribution aspects of a traditional IRA?

If you are under age 70½ and have earned income, you can contribute to this type of IRA. Here are the fundamentals:

- Contributions may be up to the lesser of $4,000 or 100% of earned income for 2006.
- Contributions for spouses who have no earned income are based on the earnings of the employed spouse. The contribution limit for the non-working spouse is also $4,000.
- Maximum contribution for married taxpayers is $8,000 or $4,000 each.
- If you are 50 or over, you are eligible for a catch-up contribution, which is an additional $1,000 in 2006.

What are the distribution rules for a traditional IRA?

Most IRA owners intend to keep their assets in the account until their retirement years, but, for various reasons, are forced to distribute the assets earlier. Distributions that occur before the age of 59½ are subject to a 10% early withdrawal penalty, in addition to any income tax, but the IRS does offer the ability to have this early-distribution penalty waived if the distributions are used for qualified reasons. Remember these options should be discussed with a qualified tax advisor:

- Qualified or unreimbursed medical expenses; also, payment for medical insurance under certain conditions
- Death or disability
- Buying a home for the first time—up to a $10,000 lifetime maximum
- As part of a Substantially Equal Payments Program (SEPP), also known as a 72(t), over the life of the IRA holder or the joint life expectancy of the IRA holder and a beneficiary, the payments must last five years or until the IRA owner reaches age 59½—whichever is longer
- For qualified higher education expenses for owner and/or dependents
- For payment of an IRS levy. The IRS may levy against an IRA, resulting in a distribution. The distributed amount is subjected to income tax, but the early distribution penalty is waived

It's important to note that distributions occurring on or after you reach 59½ may be subject to income tax, but will not be subject to any early-distribution penalty. There are also required minimum distributions that must begin no later than April 1st of the year after the IRA owner turns

70½. These distributions are taxable, and failure to take them on time will result in a tax penalty of 50%.

What is the deductibility of traditional IRA contributions?

Depending on your income, filing status and other factors, you may be able to deduct all or part of your traditional IRA contributions. And, the non-working spouse's ability to deduct his or her contribution may differ from their partner's ability to deduct.

See the below chart for various scenarios regarding the deduction of contributions to a traditional IRA. Retirement withdrawals are taxed as ordinary income, but you won't have to pay taxes on earnings while your money accumulates.

Traditional deductible IRA compensation limits[5]		
Income phase-out range for determining deductibility of traditional IRA contributions for taxpayers:		
1. Covered by an employer-sponsored plan and filing as:	2006	2005
Single	$50,000 - $60,000	$50,000 - $60,000
Married filing jointly	$75,000 - $85,000	$70,000 - $80,000
Married filing separately	$0 - $10,000	$0 - $10,000
2. Not covered by an employer-sponsored retirement plan, but filing joint return with a spouse who is covered by an employer-sponsored retirement plan.	$150,000 - $160,000	$150,000 - $160,000

Deductibility of Traditional IRA Contributions for 2005 IRA

If your spouse works and participates in an employer retirement plan:

- The working spouse's ability to deduct is phased out beginning at Modified Adjusted Gross Income (MAGI) of $75,001 for tax year 2006.

- However, the non-working spouse's ability to deduct the contribution is phased out starting at MAGI of $150,001 for tax year 2006.

Roth IRA

The Roth IRA is very similar to the traditional IRA with four important differences: you can withdraw funds income tax free at retirement. This is subject to minimum five-year holding period or age 59½, whichever is later. (See chart on page 50.) It is not tax deductible; you can still contribute after age 70½; and the eligibility phase out is between $150,000 to 160,000 for married taxpayers filing a joint return, and between $95,000 to 110,000 for single taxpayers.

The distribution and withdrawal rules are rather simple: If you take money out before a minimum five-year holding period or age 59½, whichever is later, you may owe a 10% penalty tax, as well as ordinary income

---

5 ©2006 Forefield, Inc., Used with Permission. All Rights Reserved.

tax, on all earnings that you withdraw. However, the original after-tax contribution to the Roth can be withdrawn anytime, free of penalty and taxes, and can be taken before the taxable earnings. The five-year holding period begins on January 1st of the year that the first Roth IRA account is opened. When the first account satisfies the holding period, all other Roth IRA accounts do, too.

Exceptions are the same as for the traditional IRA, however, as noted earlier, minimum distributions are required at age 70½ on the traditional IRA.

Like the traditional IRA, Roth IRAs are flexible, and they are a popular way for individuals to save for their retirement. The chart below may be useful to summarize the major points we have discussed so far. Keep in mind that you should discuss what may be the best choice for you with a qualified tax advisor.

Traditonal IRA and Roth IRA Comparison Chart[6]

	Traditional IRA	Roth IRA
Annual Contribution Limit	For 2006, $4,000 ($5,000 for those 50 and older) either deductible or non-deductible (in combination with Roth IRA)	For 2006, $4,000 ($5,000 for those 50 and older) in combination with traditional IRA.
Eligibility	Available to anyone who has earned income and is under age 70½.	Available to anyone who has earned income; single filers with AGI of $95,000 or less; joint filers with AGI of $150,000 or less.
Deductibility	Full deduction allowed if individual is not an "active participant" in an employer-sponsored retirement plan. Deductibility for active participants is determined by AGI. Non-covered spouse of active participant can deduct contribution up to $4,000 ($5,000 for those 50 and older) for 2006 subjects to AGI limit ($150,000 for joint filers)	Always non-deductible
Tax on Distributions	Distributions and earnings from a deductible IRA are taxed as ordinary income. Distributions of non-deductible contributions are considered a non-taxable return of capital.	Qualified distributions, distributions of contribution amounts and distributions of conversion amounts are tax-free. The earnings portions of non-qualified distributions are subject to income tax.
Tax or Penalty on Premature Distributions	Ordinary income tax on entire distribution: 10% penalty on distributions prior to age 59½ unless made for death or disability, first-time home purchase ($10,000 lifetime maximum), medical expenses in excess of 7.5% of AGI, certain educational expenses, to an alternate payee pursuant to a divorce decree or separation agreement, for payment of health insurance premiums during certain times of unemployment, or as part of a series of substantially equal payments based on the owner's life expectancy.	Distributions of conversion amounts made prior to five years are subject to penalty. The earnings portion of non-qualified distributions are taxable as ordinary income and subject to penalty unless made for death or disability, first-time home purchase ($10,000 lifetime maximum), medical expenses in excess of 7.5% of AGI, certain educational expenses or as part of a series of substantially equal payments based on owner's life expectancy.
Required Minimum Distributions	Must begin by April 1 of the year following the year age 70½ is attained.	Only applies to beneficiaries upon death of IRA owner.

---

6 Copyright © 2006 Raymond James Financial, Inc. All rights reserved.

Should you convert your Traditional IRA to a Roth IRA?

There is no easy answer to the Roth IRA conversion question. The conversion decision depends on a number of factors, including your tax bracket today versus what it may be tomorrow, how you will pay the taxes due on the conversion, the size of your estate, your plans for the estate as well as other factors. You should examine this issue with a qualified tax advisor using your own set of circumstances to determine whether or not the conversion is appropriate for you.

While there is no minimum or maximum amount that must be converted, on conversion any previously untaxed money in the traditional IRA must be declared as income, and it will be taxed at ordinary income tax rates.

Here are a few other factors to consider before converting over:

- You trade current income taxes for the potential of income tax free withdrawals in retirement.

- Using IRA funds to pay the conversion tax may have significant drawbacks. These funds, used to pay the tax, may themselves be subject to federal income tax. There could also be a 10% premature distribution tax if you are under 59½.

- Your modified adjusted gross income must be $100,000 or less, regardless of whether you are single or married filing a joint return. The converted amount is not included in the determination of your adjusted gross income for this calculation. (For purposes of arriving at the $100,000 figure.)

- You can make contributions to a Roth IRA after age 70½ if you have earned income.

- No minimum distributions from a Roth IRA are required after age 70½.

- You can use the Roth IRA as an estate planning tool to provide beneficiaries with tax free income. (Note: The money will come out of the IRA tax free from ordinary income tax, but not estate tax free.)

- You do not qualify for a conversion if you are married and file separate tax returns.

- Keep in mind, laws may change affecting conversion availability.

Partial Conversions

Most people will find that if a conversion makes sense, the best choice is a full conversion. But a partial conversion can be helpful in some circumstances. For example:

Tax brackets. A full conversion may cause you to report enough income to push you into a higher tax bracket. That may not always be a big concern, especially if you're moving from the 25% to the 28% bracket. But if you're moving from the 15% to the 25% bracket, that can be a pretty big tax jump. You should understand that only the portion of your taxable income that falls into the higher bracket would be subject to the higher rate. You won't pay a higher tax on all of your income merely because it pushes up into the next bracket. Still, in some cases it may make sense to limit your rollover to the amount that you can fit within your current tax bracket, especially if you're looking at the difference between the 15% and the 25% bracket.

Cash available to pay tax. You may have cash available to pay tax on a partial conversion, but not enough to pay tax on a full conversion. If you're under 59½ and you have to use some of your IRA money to pay tax on the conversion, you could end up paying a 10% early distribution tax. It may make sense to figure out how much tax you can handle without dipping into IRA assets and then figure out how much you can convert for that amount of tax.[7]

Employer Retirement Plans

For most of us, an employer-sponsored retirement plan will be the foundation of our retirement savings strategy. There are two basic types of plans: defined contribution and defined benefit. Defined contribution plans offer the opportunity to defer income, creating an investment account with tax advantages. When you invest a portion of your income in a defined contribution plan, you are normally investing pre-tax dollars, which reduces your taxable income. You can defer taxes on this account until you withdraw the money, usually after you retire, which allows your retirement account to grow even more when combined with the power of compounding. Defined benefit plans do not normally create a tax-advantaged investment account. Instead, at retirement, they offer regular monthly income that is taxed as ordinary income. While state and federal pensions offer cost-of-living adjustments (COLAs) to offset inflation, most private company plans do not offer this advantage. The major appeal of this plan is the predictability of knowing exactly what your monthly income will be, and that it is not directly dependent on any investment performance.

The majority of our focus from here forward will be on defined contribution plans for two reasons. First, defined contribution plans are more involved, at least from the employee's point of view, and require more explanation. Secondly, they are becoming the major plan of choice for most employers. Some of these plans are composed entirely of employer contributions, like profit-sharing plans, while others, such as the 401(k) plan, are composed primarily of employee contributions, often with part of the contributions matched by the employer. Your company's plan spells out who can contribute, how much, and when you can contribute. Unlike the previously mentioned defined benefit plan, the contribution amounts, not the future benefits, are set in advance. You or your employer, or both,

---

[7] Tax Guide for Investors, Fairmark Press, Fairmark Guide to the Roth IRA

contribute to your retirement account each year. The benefit amount is not guaranteed because it depends on the amounts that are contributed and how well the investments perform. You, however, have more control over both the contribution amount, as well as the types of investments you invest in.

One of the biggest advantages of a defined contribution plan is that the money you invest in a plan and the earnings on those contributions are deferred from income taxes until you withdraw the money. Since your tax bracket may well be lower when that day comes, you could experience an overall tax savings.

Some of the more common defined contribution plans are:

- 401(k) – This most popular plan is offered by for-profit companies, typically with more than 25 employees.
- 403(b) – This plan is offered by nonprofit organizations such as public schools, and state and local hospitals. The 403(b) is sometimes referred to as a TSA (tax-sheltered annuity).
- Section 457 – The defined contribution plan for state and local government employees.
- SEP-IRA – Simplified Employee Pension (SEP) plans are offered by small businesses, typically with one to 20 employees and gross revenues under $2 million. The employer makes all of the contributions to this plan, unless the plan was started before 1996 and had a salary-reduction provision.
- Simple IRA – Savings Incentive Match Plans for Employees (SIMPLE) plans offered by small businesses allow both employer and employee to make contributions. The most popular option requires employers to match employee contributions up to 3% of an employee's salary.
- Pension Plans – This is the other retirement plan, also called the defined benefit plan, mentioned earlier. Some will allow employees to take their pension as a lump-sum distribution as opposed to a monthly income.

For sake of illustration, we will now focus on the various options and features of the most popular defined contribution plan, the 401(k).

The 401(k) Plan

It is a salary-reduction plan that may be part of a profit-sharing or stock-bonus plan. It permits you to contribute before-tax dollars and reduce your taxable income, and allows your earnings to accumulate income-tax-deferred until you withdraw it at retirement. Your employer may match a certain percentage of your contributions. With 401(k)—and 403(b)—plans you have to work for an organization for a certain length of time to have rights to the company match. This is called being vested, and often it takes five years or more to become totally vested. Employee elective deferrals are always 100% vested immediately. Another feature of this plan is that the majority of the time you can select from several investment choices.

Generally speaking, if you have worked for your employer for more than one year and you are at least 21 years old, you will be allowed to participate in the plan, although your employer may offer more liberal eligibility requirements.

Annual contribution limits are as follows.[8]

- Deferrals, matching contributions, and optional profit sharing cannot exceed the lesser of either 100% of your compensation or $44,000.
- The employee's total salary deferral cannot exceed the lesser of either $15,000 for the year, or the limit set by the employer's plan for 2006[9].
- A catch-up provision is permitted if you are 50 years of age or older. The catch-up provision for 2006 is $5,000.

Mandatory required distributions begin after age 70½ unless you are still employed by the plan sponsor. Withdrawals must begin no later than April 1st of the year following the year n which you turn 70½. If you are still working for the employer sponsoring the plan, you are required to start taking distributions by April 1st of the year following the year in which you retire. The company plan must allow for this provision, and you cannot own more than five percent of the company to participate.

Many plans allow you to choose between a lump-sum payout and an annuity. As discussed earlier, there are advantages and disadvantages to both decisions, which you should discuss with your financial advisor or your CPA. If you have a financial emergency, some company plans allow for a "hardship" withdrawal. Some common qualifying reasons for such a withdrawal include paying medical expenses, avoiding foreclosure on your home, paying college tuition, and covering funeral expenses for a family member. The withdrawals are subject to income tax and, if you are under 59½, may be subject to a 10% penalty. Therefore, these funds should be used in an emergency only, and if you have no other alternative.

Your 401(k) may be the source for a loan, and remember, the principal and interest payments you pay go directly into your plan account. This means you are not only receiving your loan principal back, but you are also paying the loan interest to yourself.

Retirement income is taxed as ordinary income when withdrawn. The 10% penalty tax rules apply on all money taken out before age 59½ with a few qualified exceptions.

- Separation of service and reaching age 55

---

[8] These contribution limits are ceilings established by federal tax law. Your state or individual plan may have more restrictive limits.

[9] This amount is for 2006.

- Death
- Disability
- Rollover to an IRA
- Substantially equal payments made over your life expectancy (specific requirements apply).

Taking Your Money Out of the Plan

So, what happens to your 401(k) plan when you retire, move, or change jobs? You have the following options:

- You can leave the funds where they are, if allowed.
- You can take monthly withdrawals.
- You can transfer your plan into your new company's plan, if allowed.
- You can take company stock, if available.
- You can take a lump-sum distribution (but you should weigh rolling it into another retirement plan compared with paying taxes if you take this option).
- Your can transfer your funds into a traditional IRA (the most common option).

If you are not rolling over your 401(k) plan and decide to take a lump-sum distribution, here are a few considerations:

- You must include the entire taxable amount in your gross income for tax purposes.
- If you were born before January 1, 1936, you may be able to use the 10-year averaging rules (also called forward-averaging),[10] which may result in more favorable tax treatment.
- If you made contributions to a plan prior to 1974, these contributions may receive special capital gains treatment.
- If you are under age 59½, there will be an additional 10% early withdrawal penalty.
- The early withdrawal penalty will not apply if you are at least 55 years old and have terminated your employment.

If you were born on or after January 1, 1936 there are a few rules you need to know with regard to taking the lump-sum distribution:

- You cannot use 10-year averaging
- You cannot use capital gain treatment
- You are limited to choosing either an IRA rollover or paying ordinary income tax on this distribution

Moving Your Plan to an IRA

There are three ways to move your retirement plan to an IRA.

---

[10] Using the 1986 rates

1. Your employer can give you a check and you can put the proceeds into your IRA. This is called a rollover. This method is, generally, not preferable as it results in a 20% federal withholding requirement. (See below for more details on this option.)

2. Your employer can make a check payable to your IRA trustee and you can forward that check to the IRA trustee. This is called a direct rollover.

3. Your employer sends your retirement plan funds directly to your IRA trustee. This is called a transfer.

One important rule to understand in terms of moving a company retirement plan to an IRA is that if the check is made out to you instead of the IRA trustee (see option one above), the employer will withhold 20% of the gross proceeds. The amount withheld must be made up from your own personal savings within 60 days or it will be subject to income tax, and if you are below the age of 55 it will also be subject to a 10% penalty.

The more preferable way to move the company plan to the IRA would be to have the check made out to the IRA custodian for the benefit of the 401(k) account owner. This will result in 100% of the gross proceeds moving into the IRA.

Required Minimum Distribution (RMD) Rules on IRAs and Retirement Plans

The minimum withdrawal required from traditional IRAs and some employer plans is the result of dividing the account balance (as of the end of the preceding calendar year) by an applicable divisor provided by the IRS. The amount of the withdrawal must be recalculated each year. By taking the minimum withdrawals you can maximize the use of tax-deferred compounding.

In 2002 the IRS issued new, final regulations that dramatically changed the way RMDs are calculated. Under the new rules, there are two possible ways to calculate RMDs: the simplified general rule, or the younger spouse rule, if applicable.

The simplified general rule is the method that most IRA owners and retirement plan participants use to calculate their RMDs. It is a straightforward calculation. For each calendar year simply divide your account balance as of December 31 of the prior year, by your remaining life expectancy as determined under the Uniform Lifetime Table. This Uniform Lifetime Table allows you to use joint life expectancy based on a beneficiary who is assumed to be 10 years younger than you. This shows your life expectancy as longer, thus resulting in a smaller required minimum distribution, which results in less taxable income.

The younger spouse rule provides one exception to the simplified general rule. If your sole designated beneficiary is your spouse, and he or she is more than 10 years younger than you, the calculation of your RMD may be based on the longer joint-and-survivor life expectancy of you and your spouse. Consequently, if your spouse is your designated beneficiary, and is more than 10 years younger than you, you can take your RMDs over a longer payout period than under the Uniform Lifetime Table.

These new rules on calculating RMDs are much easier to understand than the rules that were previously enforced. They are also more advantageous to you and other IRA owners and plan participants, because they generally allow RMDs to be taken over a longer payout period. This reduces the dollar amount of the RMD, which generally reduces the tax that it triggers.

$$\frac{AB}{AD} = RMD$$	AB = Account balance at end of preceding calendar year AD = Applicable divisor RMD = Required minimum distribution for current year

If you don't take enough for the annual required amount you will be taxed a penalty of 50% of the difference between the required and actual withdrawals.

You can always take out more than the required amount, but you cannot count it toward future required distribution amounts. Say, for example, your required withdrawal this year is $1,500 but you take out $2,000. You can't carry the $500 over to count against the next year's required distribution. But, because you've reduced your IRA balance, your subsequent minimum distributions will be lower than they would have been otherwise. The IRS will let you take your required distribution in installments, but be sure that these disbursements, be they monthly, quarterly or some other increment, total at least the yearly minimum amount you're obligated to withdraw.[11]

Early Retirement Distribution Choices

If you plan to retire early, have a medical emergency or have a death in the family, you may need to tap into your retirement savings prior to age 59½. Tax laws discourage this by imposing a 10% early distribution penalty, in addition to ordinary income taxes. However, as mentioned earlier, under Internal Revenue Code, Section 72(t), penalty-free distributions prior to age 59½ are allowed as part of a series of "substantially equal periodic payments." This may help you with those income needs.

If you select the substantially equal periodic payments option, you must

---

[11] Bankrate, Inc. "Tax Tips"

follow the withdrawal schedule for either five years or until you reach age 59½, whichever is later.[12] Otherwise, the 10% penalty is applied retroactively, plus interest. Withdrawals may be modified or stopped after the minimum withdrawal period is satisfied. In order to avoid a penalty the IRS has outlined three approved methods for withdrawals in its Section 72(t):[13]

1. ***Required minimum distribution method.*** Calculates each annual distribution by dividing your IRA or retirement account balance (revalued each year) by a life expectancy factor. Because of this method, your distribution amount will vary. This choice may be for you if you are concerned about depleting the account too quickly.

2. ***Fixed amortization methods.*** This is based on a life expectancy table and a reasonable interest rate to determine principal-plus-interest payments, similar to home loan payments.[14] This method yields a fixed annual amount.

3. ***Fixed annuitization methods.*** Based on an annuity factor that uses a reasonable mortality table and interest rate.[15] It will also yield a fixed annual amount.

Determining the most appropriate withdrawal method depends on a number of factors, such as your age and account balance. Keep in mind, this can lead to a loss of principal when combined with market losses and the inability to stop the payment schedule once it has started. Be sure to talk to your financial advisor or CPA to help determine the appropriate selection for you.

Choosing Your Beneficiary

Most people name one or more of the following as beneficiaries for their IRA: spouse, children, grandchildren, a friend, a trust, a charity, or an estate. The rules regarding minimum distributions will vary depending on who the beneficiary is, so it is a good idea to check with your financial advisor, estate planning attorney, or CPA before making this important selection.

But, let's talk a little bit about the effect of some of your selections on your IRA.

If you do not designate a beneficiary, or you specify your estate as beneficiary, your IRA will go through the probate process. This can create unnecessary expense, and may cause your IRA to end up in the hands of people you did not want it to.

If you name your spouse as beneficiary, he or she can choose to continue the IRA and make required minimum withdrawals over his or her remaining life expectancy. This option may be an advantage to a surviv-

---

[12] Exceptions may apply. See Revenue Ruling 2002-62
[13] ©2006 Forefield, Inc. Used with permission. All rights reserved.
[14] IBID
[15] IBID

ing spouse who is younger than 59½, because he or she can take the distributions without paying an early withdrawal penalty. The surviving spouse can also roll it into his or her own IRA and name new beneficiaries, or select a distribution option such as taking a lump-sum amount.

If you name a beneficiary other than your spouse, that person cannot roll your IRA into his or her own IRA, but can choose to take a lump sum or select from other distribution methods including the strategy of setting up an "inherited" IRA. The inherited IRA strategy is generally preferred over the lump sum, as it can dramatically reduce the tax consequences by taking much smaller distributions over the beneficiary's life expectancy. Taking a lump sum all at once, or over a much shorter time period, will trigger a much larger amount of tax.

The Inherited IRA: Top 10 Mistakes to Avoid [16]

1. Not seeing a qualified tax or financial adisor before making your decision.

2. Not keeping current with tax law changes.

3. Having too many IRA custodians.

4. Immediately rolling over money to the spouses' IRA.

5. Rolling over an IRA when it is not allowed.

6. Taking the money from the IRA instead of properly establishing an inherited IRA.

7. Not establishing the Inherited IRA properly.

8. Improper funding of exemption trust, marital trust, Q-tip trusts or any other trust.

9. Waiting until the last minute to make changes on the IRA.

10. Not reviewing the cost before splitting into inherited IRAs.

If you choose a trust as beneficiary, it gives you maximum control over such things as who receives IRA funds, when they receive them, and even what type of investments can be used. It can also help you save estate taxes in certain situations, if set up properly. The main disadvantages of using a trust as your beneficiary are the trust must use the life expectancy of the oldest trust beneficiary when calculating minimum distributions, unless the trust document allows otherwise (which most do not); and some IRA custodians will not "look through" the trust to allow certain elections.

If you choose your favorite charity as your beneficiary, the charity pays no income tax on receipt of the funds, and these assets are not included in your taxable estate, thus reducing potential estate tax. The main disadvantages of choosing a charity as your beneficiary are that it does not give you an income tax deduction — since

---

[16] Thomas B Gau and Robert S Keebler

the IRA funds are not transferred to the charity until after your death, and there could be possible erosion of the planned gift to the charity due to required minimum distributions.

A Last Word

If you are approaching retirement, you'll soon be making some very complex financial decisions. It is important to make the appropriate choices based on your personal circumstances and savings, your company retirement plan, and government-sponsored programs. Failure to consider all options and make the correct decision could cause you to give part of your retirement money away to pay taxes and penalties, many of which can be avoided with proper planning.

The complexity of various retirement plans has increased significantly over the past few years and it's important to be counseled properly by a skilled financial advisor or accounting professional. I hope this chapter will be helpful in guiding you to make the most of your retirement dollars.

◆◆◆

Mike Piershale, Registered Principal, Raymond James Financial Services, Inc., holds a master's degree in business education from the University of Missouri. After teaching business courses for four years, he entered the financial services industry in 1983. With more than 20 years of experience, Mike has extensive training in all areas of financial planning.

Mike is ranked in the top one percent of financial advisors with Raymond James Financial Services, and is their top-ranked financial advisor in Illinois. He is also a member of the distinguished Chairman's Council with Raymond James, a distinction awarded to only the top advisors nationwide. Mike has been featured in *Barron's* and the *Wall Street Journal,* in the prestigious RJ Shook Winner's Circle representing the top financial advisors in the United States, and in the book *The Trust Equation: A Consumer Guide to Finding a Competent and Ethical Financial Advisor* by Steven Drozdeck.

Mike can be reached at Raymond James Financial Services, Inc. 4318 W. Crystal Lake Road, Unit H, McHenry, Illinois 60050; (tel) 815.363.3368; (email) mike. piershale@raymondjames.com.

Life Insurance
Needs of the Retiree

Charlie "Bubba" Meagher, President
Meagher Financial Services, Inc.

Does life insurance have a role in your retirement financial plan? In this chapter, we will discuss five situations involving life insurance during retirement:

- When Your Group Life Insurance Ends
- Using Life Insurance to Maximize Your Pension Income
- Long-Term Care Life Insurance Combination (Either Way You Get A Benefit)
- The Cheapest Way to Pay Estate Taxes
- What to Do with the Life Insurance Policy You No Longer Need

When Your Group Life Insurance Ends

Most group life insurance plans terminate or are significantly reduced at retirement, and then eliminated at age 70. That is one of the reasons group term life is inexpensive. Relatively few benefits are paid. Most of us want to have some life insurance benefit paid to our families when we die. Funeral costs, uninsured medical expenses, debt repayment, tax payment, and income for surviving family members are reasons we want life insurance.

What will life insurance cost if you wait until you lose your group life insurance to buy new coverage? Should you buy term insurance or should you buy permanent insurance? On the next page is a chart illustrating what $100,000 of 20-year term insurance would cost annually at different ages.

Remember, if you live longer than the 20 years

20-Year Term Insurance $100,000		
AGE	MALE	FEMALE
55	$436	$329
60	$673	$493
65	$1,319	$850
70	$2,209	$1,431

your 20-year term life insurance will not pay a benefit. Life expectancy for people attaining age 65 is 84.8 for women and 80.9 for men. That is why most people want permanent insurance. Because it is guaranteed to be in-force regardless of how long you live. This chart illustrates what you can expect to pay annually for a $100,000 policy guaranteed to stay in-force until you die.

Low-Cost, No-Lapse $100,000 Universal Life		
AGE	MALE	FEMALE
55	$1,159	$941
60	$1,567	$1,249
65	$2,140	$1,720
70	$3,211	$2,561

Life insurance is still a valuable asset because it provides money when money is needed most. Consider the cost of waiting until your group life insurance expires, and you may want to purchase life insurance before your retirement day.

Using Life Insurance to Maximize Your Pension Income

Planning for retirement has never been a more critical issue than it is today. Independent studies from numerous sources indicate that a frightening number of Americans are woefully under-prepared for a financially secure retirement. Traditional financial planning regards retirement income as a three-legged stool. One leg is Social Security benefits. The second includes personal savings and investments, and the third is the employer-sponsored qualified retirement plan. Needless to say, the future of the Social Security system is currently the subject of fierce political debate, and personal savings rates are at near historic lows.

Background – Every married retiree who participates in a qualified retirement plan will be faced with an important economic decision. Before retirement, every worker should carefully consider the payout options from their plan in order to make an informed decision. Current law requires that a pension plan automatically provide a participating employee with a qualified joint and survivor annuity as a payout option. This is to ensure that a surviving spouse continues to receive a lifetime retirement benefit in the event of the retiree's death. However, providing this ongoing survivorship benefit is a very expensive proposition, because it results in a substantial decrease in the monthly benefit paid to the retiring worker and, ultimately, to the surviving spouse. Nevertheless, many retirees will opt for this reduced pension amount to guarantee a survivor income for his or her spouse.

The Problem – There are several distinct disadvantages of choosing a joint and survivor payout. The first and most obvious disadvantage is the reduced monthly benefit for the retiree in order to provide for a contingency that might not even happen, mainly the survival of the spouse. Once made, the retirement payout decision is most often irrevocable. It cannot be changed if the retiree's spouse dies first. You might note that there are a few plans that allow for a pop-up provision, allowing benefits to increase for the retiree upon the spouse's death, but these plans are not common. Thus, in the event of the spouse's death, the retiree is locked into a much lower pension benefit for life. Further, if both spouses die within a relatively short amount of time, the benefit plan ceases entirely and surviving heirs will likely receive nothing. This should not be the end result of a lifetime of hard work.

The Solution – Pension maximization is a way to increase the pension income for retired workers while, at the same time, providing crucial on-going benefits to the surviving spouse in the event of the retiree's death. This involves taking a full single-life benefit from the pension plan rather than a reduced joint-life benefit. The worker's spouse must consent to this election in writing. This provides a higher monthly retirement benefit, but it ends when the participant dies. Under the pension maximization approach, the surviving spouse's retirement income is derived from the life insurance on the participant. At death, these life insurance proceeds may be annuitized for the surviving spouse, or may be invested in a separate account and drawn down as needed by the survivor to support his or her retirement income needs. If the pension maximization plan is structured correctly and funded with an adequate amount of life insurance, both spouses may benefit from higher levels of retirement income over any of the possible joint and survivor options.

The concept of pension maximization is really just part of an overall retirement planning strategy. It should be carefully considered and implemented in concert with all other retirement vehicles and techniques.

How Pension Maximization Works

This approach allows retirees to enjoy the full benefits of a pension while simultaneously providing a life income for the survivor's spouse.

Step 1. In planning for retirement, the worker purchases an adequate amount of life insurance and names the spouse as beneficiary. The earlier the life insurance purchase, the better.

Step 2. At retirement, the worker chooses the full life income option from the pension plan, maximizing the monthly benefit.

Step 3. If the retired worker dies first, the spouse can continue to receive income from the policy death benefits.

Step 4. If the spouse dies first, the retiree will not only continue to receive the full pension benefit, but will also own a valuable asset in the form of life insurance. At this point, (the death of the spouse) the retiree has a number of favorable financial options:

a) Keep the policy in force with new beneficiaries, perhaps the children, creating an income tax-free inheritance.

b) Convert the policy's cash value into an additional stream of lifetime income.

c) Keep the policy in force and withdraw or borrow cash value as needed to supplement retirement income.

d) Convert the policy to a reduced paid-up insurance and designate a new beneficiary.

e) Retirees who remarry may use this life insurance to help provide benefits for a new spouse.

f) Policy ownership has many other possible benefits in addition to the pension maximization use such as collateral for loan, estate liquidity and charitable giving.

Tax Considerations – Payments made to retired workers are fully taxable when all contributions to the plan have been made by the employer. Insurance policy death benefits paid as a lump sum, on the other hand, are not taxable as income to the beneficiary. Generally, the interest earned on proceeds held by the insurer under a settlement option is taxable as it is received. Death benefits taken over a period of time as an annuity are taxable only to the extent that an annuity payment is deemed to represent income. A certain portion of each payment is considered as return of capital. The taxable portion of each payment is calculated by applying an appropriate exclusion ratio. This ratio reflects the portion of yearly annuity payments that can be excluded from gross income.

Summary – The pension maximization concept is a valuable technique for married workers who are in reasonably good health and are covered by an employer-sponsored pension plan. It most often should be considered in conjunction with other elements of the overall retirement planning process to maximize the total retirement income available to both spouses. Structured properly and with adequate life insurance, pension maximization may offer the greatest pension income available to a retiring worker while providing financial assurance to a surviving spouse once that retiree dies.

Let's look at a sample case to see how the cost and benefits compare with various retirement options. In the hypothetical situation featured in the chart below, a male worker is retiring at 65 with a defined-benefit pension plan. His wife is 62. Their tax bracket is 31 percent.

Cost of Traditional Pension Options						
Monthly	Life Income (1) Benefit	Joint & Equal (2) Benefit	Loss	Joint & Half (3) Benefit	Loss
Before Tax	$4,000	$3,000	$1,000	$3,320	$680
After Tax	$2,760	$2,070	$690	$2,291	$469

Retiree: Male, Age 65
Spouse: Female, Age 62
Tax Bracket: 31%

(1)   Life Income Annuity offers highest benefit ($4,000) but *ceases* when retiree dies. No benefit to surviving spouse.
(2)   Joint & Equal Annuity pays $3,000 for the lives of *both* spouses.
(3)   Joint & Half Annuity pays $3,320 while retiree, is alive; pays surviving spouse $1,660 after the retiree dies.

Pension Maximization Numbers in Action – Joint and Equal Option
Face amount of insurance to produce $3,000 monthly survivor income: **$450,000.**
(Assumes retirement at age 65, and the spouse is age 62.)

Advantage with No-Lapse Guarantee Insurance to Age 100			
Status: Male Preferred Non-Tobacco	Monthly Premium	Lifetime Income	Monthly Increase Retirement Income
Age 50	$356	$4,000	+$644
Age 55	$451	$4,000	+$549
Age 60	$565	$4,000	+$435
Age 65	$749	$4,000	+$251

Monthly Benefit Increase at Age 65 from Life Income Options: **$1,000**

(1)   If the *spouse* dies the cash value of the policy represents *additional retirement savings* available to him. He *continues* to receive maximum (life income) benefit for life.
(2)   If the *retiree* dies, the death benefit payable to the spouse represents a double-digit, tax-free *return.*

Long-Term Care Life Insurance Combination: Either Way You Get a Benefit

Retirees should start planning for long-term care when they are still active and healthy. Long-term care is expensive. Adequate long-term care insurance can preserve the retiree's assets and their quality of life. One year in a nursing home or 24-hour home care can cost more than $66,000 today. Long-term care costs have been increasing at about four percent per year. This could cost $150,000-250,000 per year in 20-30 years. Sixty percent of retirees reaching age 65 will need long-term care at some point in their lives.

The Problem – Retirees face the dilemma of providing for their long-term care needs. Do they spend their assets or buy insurance to cover their expenses and preserve their assets? Traditional long-term care insurance works similar to auto insurance. You pay a premium and select a deductible, and benefit amount. You collect the benefit only if you have a wreck. With traditional long-term care insurance, you select deductible and benefit amounts, pay a premium, and collect only if you need long-term care. If you are among the 40 percent who will not need long-term care, all the premiums you pay will be lost.

The Solution – The combination of life insurance and long-term care insurance offers a cost-efficient, convenient way to help you plan for your future. When retirees choose this option, their policy's entire death benefit is available for a long-term care benefit. You can use all, some or none of your death benefit to pay for long-term care expenses. The choice is yours. Any portion you don't use will be paid to your heirs and will be income-tax favored under current law.

Steps to implement the long-term care combination:

1. Choose the type and amount of life insurance you want. The insurance industry offers whole life, universal life, variable universal life and indexed life insurance policies to combine with long-term care benefits.

2. Choose a long-term care benefit amount. Typically, your long-term care monthly benefit will be your choice of one to four percent of the life insurance policy's face amount.

3. Choose your funding or premium-paying period. Most insurance companies offering this combination protection allow you to pay/fund in a lump sum, single premium, for a limited number of years or over your entire lifetime.

Now, you have many options:

A. Benefit protection

The full amount of your life insurance death benefit is your total benefit pool, which is available for both life insurance and long-term care protection.

B. Benefit flexibility

You may use all, some, or none of your total benefit pool to pay for long-term care costs. The choice is yours.

C. Benefit assurance

That portion of your total benefit pool not used for long-term care purposes will be paid to your heirs as a death benefit, income-tax favored under current tax law.

D. Growth of Guarantees

Depending on the type of life insurance you purchase, your policy will offer either a guaranteed death benefit, total benefit pool or it will offer the potential to grow the account value by the total benefit pool. The chart below illustrates how the combination life insurance, long-term care sets up a "benefit pool."

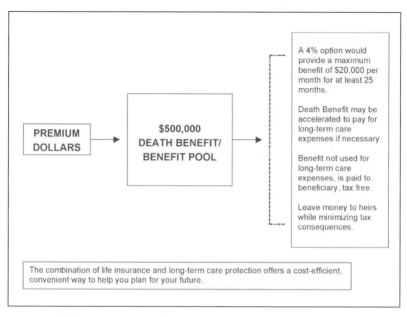

• A four-percent option would provide a maximum benefit of $20,000 per month for at least 25 months.

• Death benefit may be accelerated to pay for long-term care expenses if necessary.

• Benefit not used for long-term care expenses is paid to beneficiary tax free.

• Leave money to heirs while minimizing tax consequences.

• The combination of life insurance and long-term care protection offers a cost-efficient, convenient way to help you plan for your future.

Summary – The life/long-term care combination plan gives retirees a cost-efficient, convenient way to provide themselves with a better quality of life while protecting their assets. Unlike traditional stand-alone long-term care, the life insurance long-term care combination guarantees your money back.

The Cheapest Way to Pay Estate Taxes

Other chapters in this book will look at estate planning techniques and the use of life insurance as an inexpensive way to pay estate tax liabilities and preserve assets for your family. Therefore, a limited discussion is provided here.

Estate taxes can be paid in a variety of ways:

1. ***Using cash in an estate***. The problem is this decreases the value of the estate left to heirs.

2. ***Selling assets in an estate to pay estate tax liabilities.*** Often, the forced sale of assets like real estate, stocks, or a business results in a reduction of the asset's value, making the total cost to the estate even more expensive.

3. ***Borrowing money to pay estate taxes.*** Here the total cost to the estate is even greater because the cost is the tax rate plus the interest rate.

4. ***Purchasing life insurance to pay for estate tax liabilities.*** This method often proves to be the most cost-efficient way to pay estate taxes. Taxes can be paid with pennies on the dollar. The life insurance premium is usually less expensive than the interest a family would have to pay by borrowing the money.

The estate tax table below shows how current law is taxing the estates. Look at what happens in the year 2011*. Estate taxes go back up significantly.

Summary – Estate planning and preservation should include an examination of life insurance as a means of paying estate tax expenses and preserving estate assets.

Death in Year	Exclusion	Highest Rate Starts at Taxable	Highest Rate
2002	$1,000,000	$2,500,000	50%
2003	$1,000,000	$2,000,000	49%
2004	$1,500,000	$2,000,000	48%
2005	$1,500,000	$2,000,000	47%
2006	$2,000,000	$2,000,000	46%
2007 & 2008	$2,000,000	$1,500,000	45%
2009	$3,500,000	$1,500,000	45%
2010	$00	No Tax	No Tax
*2011	$1,000,000	$3,000,000	55%

What to Do with the Life-Insurance Policy
You No Longer Need: Life Settlements

Some retirees find they own life insurance they no longer need or can't afford. Large life insurance policies have been purchased to pay anticipated estate taxes. Tax law changes and asset erosion may now make the life insurance unnecessary (see the estate-tax table). Additionally, businesses may have owned a life insurance policy on a key employee or a business owner that is no longer needed because of retirement or the sale of a business. When a retiree finds they no longer need or can't afford their policy, the decision of what to do with the policy needs to be made.

1. Cancel it for its cash value, if any.

2. Take a reduced paid up policy.

3. Exercise the extended term provision.

4. Sell it in the secondary (or life settlement) insurance market.

The secondary life insurance market has been growing significantly in the past decade. Large institutional investors, hedge funds, and other savvy investors are buying unwanted life insurance policies. They are especially interested in large policies owned by people over 65. If the insured has had a negative health change since the policy's inception, the policy will be even more valuable. A term insurance policy that can be converted to a permanent policy could also be sold in the life settlement market. This chart shows actual examples of insurance policy sales on the life-settlement secondary market.

Insured Age	Policy Face	Cash to Policyholder If Surrendered to Insurance Company	Cash received in Life Settlement Sale	Gain With Settlement
M 81	$250,000	$54,000	$62,500	$8,500
F 85	$600,000	$5,000	$260,000	$255,000
F 78	$2,000,000	$18,000	$140,000	$122,000
*M 71	$7,500,000	0	$224,000	$224,000
*M75	$11,000,000	$265,000	$2,750,000	$2,485,000

*Insured used part of sale proceeds to purchase a better new policy.

Life settlements have risk. Once the policy is sold, the death benefit is lost. Insurance companies have a maximum amount of insurance they are willing to issue on anyone's life. Let's suppose the maximum insurance that can be issued on your life is $5 million. If you sell an insurance policy for $2 million in the life settlement market, you would only have $3 million of insurability left. If life expectancy is very short, other assets might be better to liquidate.

Summary

Changing needs, changes in financial circumstances, changes in tax law and changes in family structure could make a life settlement very attractive. The life settlement market has made the life insurance policy an even more attractive financial instrument than ever before.

◆◆◆

Charlie "Bubba" Meagher entered the financial services industry in 1966, while still a senior at Louisiana State University, and earned his first securities license in 1969. After college, he founded Financial Concepts and Designs (FCD), a company that grew to include 3,000 registered insurance and securities representatives operating across the southeastern United States. FCD specialized in executive compensation and employee-benefit plans for clients that included some of the largest privately held companies in the southeastern region. Bubba attributes his success to the concept of a one-stop financial services team, created when he founded Meagher Financial Services, Inc. With 39 years experience, Meagher Financial Services helps clients get their legal, investment, and insurance houses in order. Bubba is a public speaker and contributes regularly to several financial publications. A Certified Estate Planner, Certified Senior Advisor, and a Registered Representative with the NASD, under the broker-dealer Resource Horizons Group, LLC, he has completed Series 6, 7, 24, 63, and 65 examinations and is a member of the Financial Planning Association.

Bubba and his wife, Debbie, are active in the Mount Bethel United Methodist Church in Marietta, Georgia, and are enthusiastic supporters of the United Way and the Hospice care organizations in the Atlanta area.

Bubba Meagher can be reached at Meagher Financial Services, Inc., 1350 Church Street Extension, 3rd Fl., Marietta, GA 30060; (tel) 770.319.1970; (email) bubba@meagherfinancial.com; (website) www.meagherfinancialservices.com.

Annuities in Action:
Your Retirement Income Assured

Arnie Pechler, Managing Partner
United Professional Advisors

"I keep six honest serving-men.
They taught me all I knew.
Their names are What and
Why and When and How
and Where and Who."

— Rudyard Kipling,
The Elephant's Child, 1902

To understand the important role of annuities in providing a secure retirement plan, I will employ the above tool, or quote of Rudyard Kipling's.

What is an Annuity?

An annuity is a contract between an individual (you become the "annuitant") and an insurance company. These are called "commercial" annuities. You will pay the insurance company a single payment or a series of payments, and the insurance company agrees to pay you an income, starting immediately or at a later date, for a specified time period. Under current tax law, the money you put into an annuity grows on a tax-deferred basis until you begin receiving the accumulated funds as income. That means that all of your earnings are reinvested in an annuity and allowed to compound without having to pay taxes on earnings.

In this chapter we will examine only commercial annuities. A limited number of annuities are issued by charitable institutions and private individuals, but for purposes of our discussion we will limit the subject to what is most applicable to you.

Let's begin with a little history. Annuities are not new; they were used in the Greek and Roman empires to solve the same problem that exists for us today. Back then, just as today, no one individual knew how long he or she would live, and no one wanted to run out of assets before they died. Annuities are uniquely suited for this situation. They were sold commercially in the United States in the early 1900s and account for more than three trillion dollars of invested assets today.

What are Their Differences?

The method by which payments are received differentiate immediate annuities and deferred annuities from some of the other types of annuities. For example:

Immediate annuities are designed so that a single sum of money is deposited with an insurance company in exchange for a series of payments, which begin immediately. These payments may be for a specified period up to, and including, the death of the annuitant. A common example of immediate annuities would be the life with 10-year period-certain option. This option stipulates that the annuitant would receive income from their contract as long as they live, however if they die during the first 10 years, their beneficiary would receive the remaining payments for the balance of the 10-year period. (See chart on page 75.)

Deferred annuities are designed to receive either single premiums, or ongoing payments into a contract for the purpose of accumulating funds for future use. When the funds are needed, the contract can be annuitized, or turned into a stream of payments, much the same as an immediate annuity. This is called the distribution phase. Another option is to surrender the contract for cash or take partial withdrawals. (See chart on page 76.)

What are the Basic Types of Deferred Annuities?

There are two basic types of deferred annuities: fixed and variable.

Fixed annuities are invested primarily in government securities and high-grade corporate bonds. They offer a guaranteed rate, typically over a period of one to 10 years.

Variable annuities enable you to invest in a selection of sub-accounts, such as securities portfolios, fixed interest accounts, and money market securities. These sub-accounts are tied to market performance, and often have a corresponding managed investment portfolio after which they are modeled.

What Deferred Annuity Income Options Are Available at Retirement?

At retirement, annuity income can be structured in a variety of ways, enabling you to select the income option that best satisfies your unique needs. While you can surrender a deferred annuity and receive a **lump-sum payment** equal to the annuity value, many people elect to convert the annuity value into a stream of retirement income:

Life Income Option	➤ Payments are made for as long as the annuitant is alive. ➤ Payments cease at the annuitant's death. ➤ This option produces the maximum guaranteed* lifetime income.
Life Income with Period Certain Option	➤ Payments are made for as long as the annuitant is alive. ➤ If the annuitant dies before a specified number of payments have been received (e.g., 120 monthly payments), the remaining payments in the period certain are made to the beneficiary.
Life Income with Refund Guarantee Option	➤ Payments are made for as long as the annuitant is alive. ➤ If the annuitant dies before payments equal to all or a specified portion of the purchase price have been received, the beneficiary receives the balance of the payments, up to the refund guarantee* amount.
Joint-and-Survivor Option	➤ This payout option covers two lives. ➤ The same payment can be received for as long as either of the two annuitants is alive or, alternatively, at the death of the first annuitant, the payment to the surviving annuitant can be structured to reduce to a specified percentage (e.g., 75%) of the payment received while both annuitants were alive. ➤ A joint-and-survivor payout can also include a period certain feature.
Period Certain Option (no guarantee of lifetime income)	➤ Payments are made for a specified number of years, such as 10 years or 20 years. ➤ Payments cease at the end of the period certain. ➤ If annuitant dies before receiving all guaranteed* payments, the beneficiary will receive the remaining payments.

*   All guarantees are based on the claims-paying ability of the issuing company.

Elements of Annuities

The major parties to an annuity contract are the issuer, annuitant, owner, and beneficiary. Here are the brief descriptions of each:

- The issuer of the annuity is an insurance company. It is important that this company is financially sound—AM Best rating of A or better—and committed to quality customer service, and the annuity business.

- The annuitant is the individual person, or persons, in the case of a joint annuity whose life is used to determine the duration of payments.

- The owner is the person, persons, or entity entitled to ownership rights under the contract. The owner may be—and usually is—the same as the annuitant, however, sometimes depending on planning strategies it may be another person, or entity such as charity.

- There are two types of beneficiaries, primary and contingent. The primary beneficiary is the person, persons, or entity to whom the benefits are payable upon death of the owner or, under certain circumstances,

73

death of the annuitant. The contingent beneficiary becomes entitled to receive the proceeds if all primary beneficiaries have died before the annuitant or owner.

Fixed Interest Annuities vs. Variable Annuities vs. Indexed Annuities

	Fixed Interest Annuities	Variable Annuities	Indexed Annuities
Minimum guaranteed return?	Yes [1]	No [2]	Yes [1]
Choice of investment options?	No	Yes	No
Opportunity to earn a higher return?	No	Yes	Yes
Possibility of losing principal?	No [1]	Yes	Maybe [3]
Tax-deferred growth?	Yes	Yes	Yes
Minimum death benefit?	Yes [1]	Yes [1]	Yes [1]

[1]   Subject to the claims-paying ability of the issuing company.
[2]   Unless 100% of premiums are placed in a guaranteed fixed interest subaccount.
[3]   It is possible to lose principal in an indexed annuity if, for example, no index-linked interest is credited to the contract because the index linked to the annuity declines or if an indexed annuity is surrendered before maturity.

Immediate Annuities vs. Deferred Annuities

	Immediate Annuities	Deferred Annuities
Premium payments?	Single premium only.	Either a single premium or a series of installment premiums.
Annuity payout?	Begins immediately or shortly after premium is paid.	Begins at a future annuity payout date, providing time for annuity accumulation.
Partial withdrawals?	No, partial withdrawals cannot be made from an immediate annuity.	Yes, subject to the terms of the contract and possible charges, partial withdrawals can be made from a deferred annuity; partial withdrawals may be subject to a premature withdrawal tax if made prior to age 59-1/2. Withdrawals will reduce the value of the death benefit and any optional benefits.
Surrender value?	None; the contract cannot be surrendered.	Yes, a deferred annuity can be surrendered for its value, subject to surrender charges and a possible premature withdrawal tax if surrendered prior to age 59-1/2.

The choice of ownership and beneficiary designations is very important and can have far-reaching consequences. Be sure to work with a competent professional when making these decisions.

Annuities Have Living Benefits, Too!

Annuities have both living benefits and death benefits. We discussed earlier that an immediate annuity could be structured to provide a series of guaranteed payments for a specific duration up to the lifetime of one or more annuitants. Our chart demonstrates average life expectancies and points out the risk of outliving your retirement income. This traditional use of annuities provides great peace of mind for

How Long Can You Expect to Live After Retirement?

Advances in medical science and healthier lifestyles
have resulted in longer life expectancies.

Male Life Expectancy		Female Life Expectancy	
Current Age	Life Expectancy (in years)	Current Age	Life Expectancy (in years)
60	20.64	60	24.08
61	19.85	61	23.27
62	19.06	62	22.47
63	18.29	63	21.68
64	17.54	64	20.90
65	16.80	65	20.12
66	16.08	66	19.36
67	15.37	67	18.60
68	14.68	68	17.86
69	13.99	69	17.12
70	13.32	70	16.40
71	12.66	71	15.69
72	12.01	72	14.99
73	11.39	73	14.31
74	10.78	74	13.64
75	10.18	75	12.98

Source: 2001 Commissioners' Standard Ordinary Mortality Table; based on composite data (combination of smokers, nonsmokers and smoking status unknown); age nearest birthday

With longer life expectancies, however, comes the
increased risk of outliving your retirement income!

our increasing longevity, along with some significant tax benefits. (See chart above.)

A 68-year-old widowed client of mine had $400,000 of investable assets, mostly in certificates of deposit, with a need for $1,350 per month of income from those investments. Income from a non-qualified or after-tax annuity is taxed under an exclusion-ratio formula, which means that a portion of the income each month is attributed to the return of principal and not taxed. So, we repositioned $200,000 into an immediate annuity with a "life and 10-year-certain" payout. In this case, 65 percent of my client's monthly income is being received income tax free and only 35 percent is taxable.

We were able to reposition some of her assets to a deferred annuity and some to other tax-favored investments and significantly increase her net cash flow. This can be a powerful strategy when applied appropriately.

Deferred annuities have several living benefits, which can be designed to meet the client's needs.

Here are some of the most common benefits, but remember that innovations and nuances occur on a regular basis so, again, it's a good idea to consult with your financial advisor from time to time about your annuity investments.

The first feature of a deferred annuity is the opportunity to grow assets on a tax-favored basis. The growth within an annuity is deferred until withdrawn.

Within a *fixed deferred annuity* this growth happens on two levels. Every fixed annuity has a lifetime contract guarantee—usually around three percent. In addition to the guarantee, companies may pay excess interest rates depending on their portfolio rates of return and their commitment to the policyholder. Generally, insurance companies use bond investments to support their crediting strategies with traditional fixed deferred annuities. They determine their portfolio yield and subtract their profit margin to determine a reasonable crediting rate. These rates are generally comparable to Certificate of Deposit rates; however, in a rapidly rising interest rate environment CDs may yield higher than annuities, and in a flat or declining interest rate environment annuities will often outpace CDs.

Some fixed annuities will offer a bonus interest rate in the first year. Be careful. Be sure you know what the base rate is and get a copy of their interest-crediting rate history; this will give you a more reasonable expectation of rate going forward.

Equity indexed annuities, because they are a variation of a fixed annuity, behave much like a fixed annuity on the guaranteed side. However, instead of the excess interest earning potential coming from the company's investment performance, it is linked to one or more market indexes like the Standard & Poor's 500, NASDAQ or Dow Jones Industrial Index.

At this point it is important to understand the following three terms which pertain to Equity Indexed Annuities:

1. *Participation Rate:* A limit on the amount of the index gain credited to your annuity. If you have a 70% participation rate and your index rises 10%, your annuity would be credited 7%.

2. *Cap Rate:* A limit set as to the maximum gain your contract can be credited in a given year. A 12% cap means if your participation rate in the index were 15% you would be limited to 12%.

3. *Spread Fee* (or Index Margin): A charge usually 1-2%. In this example if the index earns 10% and your contract has a 2% margin your return would be 8%.

Many of these provisions are adjusted at the contract anniversary date so it is important that you and your advisor pay attention!

Fixed annuities are designed to have contract guarantees, which protect your principal regardless of market performance.

Fixed Annuities

Fixed annuities are contracts under which the insurance company credits guaranteed interest rates. The assets of the issuing company back these investments, which is also responsible for the investment strategy. (Note: Variable annuity cash surrender values and income benefits are not guaranteed by the insurance company. These investments are held in separate, segregated accounts and the investments return are based on the performance of these sub-accounts. Many insurance companies now provide guaranteed minimum benefits within variable accounts, which we will discuss in further detail later in this chapter.)

Equity indexed annuities are a recent type of fixed annuity contract, which is somewhat of a hybrid. It has a fixed guarantee rate of interest with excess performance potential coming from participation in a part of the gain of a particular equity index such as the S&P 500 or Nasdaq 100. (Note: A market index tracks the performance of a specific group of stocks representing a particular segment of the market, or in some cases an entire market. For example, the S&P 500 Composite Stock Price Index is an index of 500 stocks intended to be representative of a broad segment of the market. There are indexes for almost every conceivable sector of the stock market. Most EIAs are based on the S&P 500, but other indexes also are used. Some EIAs even allow investors to select one or more indexes.)

Variable Annuities

Variable annuities provide a different component for asset growth. With this product, the contract holder has a much more active role in directing their premium contributions into a variety of sub-accounts. However, unlike a fixed annuity, amounts that are accumulated in the surrender value or income payments are not guaranteed by the insurance company. The performance of a variable annuity depends on the performance of the underlying securities, which are usually mutual-fund based. Because of this, variable annuities are subject to federal securities laws in addition to state insurance laws. You must remember there is a risk of losing money with this type of investment.

Variable annuities have two types of expense charges, which are subtracted from the investment return. Investment management expenses vary depending on the nature of sub-account investments and average between .6-1.2%. The second charge is a mortality and expense (M&E) charge, which compensates the insurance company for death benefit guarantees and the guarantee that expenses and fees will not increase during the entire life of the contract. These charges range generally between .6-1.5%. In general, these charges combined range from 1-3% depending on the options included.

Now that we are accumulating money nicely in our annuity, let's see how we can access it.

Accessing Your Money

The first — and probably the most obvious — way to access money from an annuity is to annuitize it, which means turning all or part of it into an immediate annuity. This strategy was demonstrated earlier in the client example.

Another option is to surrender the contract. This triggers two potential problems: possible surrender charges and income taxation. Most annuities sold today do not have front-end loads or sales charges; however, many do have "contingent deferred sales charges" better known as surrender penalties. These penalties can range from zero years to 20 years, on a declining basis. A common example would be a seven-year surrender charge starting at 7% in year one declining to 1% in year seven and no surrender charge thereafter.

Any gain in the value of the contract would be taxed at ordinary income tax rates in the year from which it is received. There is also a 10% penalty tax on the taxable portion of non-qualified annuity payments received prior to age 59½. These penalties are waived for qualifying disabilities, death of the contract holder, and substantially equal periodic payments over the life of the contract holder.

Another option is to take partial withdrawals from the contract. Most annuities allow 10% per year of the contract value to be withdrawn without a surrender charge. Remember that any gain is just taxed in the year from which it is withdrawn unless the contract was purchased before August 14, 1982.

Another way to move money out of an annuity contract is to exchange it free of income tax via a process commonly referred to as a 1035 Exchange. This process allows a contract holder to carry-forward loss or gain from one annuity contract to another. This process could be done if a person is not satisfied with his or her existing contract and wants to exchange to a new contract. Once again, make sure you are working with a financial professional who is experienced, skilled, and has your best interests in mind. The exchange must be a "like kind" transfer, into a new (not existing) contract and be on the same person or persons.

These exchanges often make sense; however, be sure you and your advisor understand what you may be giving up.

At death, annuity proceeds can be paid in a lump sum. Any gain received by the beneficiary above the contract holder's cost basis would be taxed as ordinary income in the year that it is received. If the beneficiary is the surviving spouse and the contract allows for the continuation with the spouse as successor-owner, the contract may be continued and taxation postponed. If the beneficiary is an individual (not an entity) he or she may receive the contract proceeds over his or her life expectancy and be taxed accordingly.

It is very important when you are considering an annuity contract that you understand how the death benefit works.

It is very important when you are considering an annuity contract that you understand how the death benefit works. Are surrender charges waived at death? If it is a variable annuity, does it offer highest anniversary value as a death benefit?

More Advantages of Annuities

Why is an annuity an investment vehicle worthy of your consideration?

The first advantage is guarantees, which are especially important in these changing times. No other financial product can guarantee an income that you cannot outlive even if you make it to 120!

Fixed annuities also provide lifetime accumulation value guarantees, which we covered earlier. Taking the possibility of loss out of an investment portfolio is extremely important. In my retirement planning seminars I often ask the question, "if you experienced a 20% loss in your investment portfolio what would you have to earn back to break even?" Most people say 20%; the correct answer is 25%. If you lose 50% the correct answer is 100% to break even. In the proverbial story of the tortoise and the hare, fixed annuities are the tortoise. When we are nearing or in retirement it is not wise to gamble all of our money on the hare.

Recent innovations to variable annuities also can provide withdrawal guarantees assuring that if 5% annual withdrawals are taken from an existing account balance that this level of withdrawals can be taken for the lifetime of the annuitant even if the underlying account value is exhausted. It is not required that the contract be annuitized to provide this benefit.

Death benefit guarantees can also be very valuable particularly with variable annuities. The standard option is that the greater of purchase payments minus withdrawals (if any) or current account value is paid at death. However, most contacts offer a highest anniversary value death benefit or periodic step-ups in death benefit at specific intervals such as every three years. This can be especially important in a sustained down market and can be a very meaningful benefit to your beneficiaries.

The second advantage is tax-deferred growth within the annuity. This can be very powerful because you are not paying current income tax on the growth in your account until the gain is withdrawn. Remember also the annuity exclusion ratio we referred to earlier in the client example.

A *third advantage of annuities is that unlike cash, mutual funds or stocks they do not pass through probate at death if they are paid to a named beneficiary.* This enables 100% of the proceeds to be paid quickly and privately.

The fourth major advantage is investment expertise. In the fixed annuity arena, professional money managers at insurance companies are managing primarily a bond portfolio which gives you not only your base lifetime guarantee, but also participation in either market indexes or excess interest crediting to your account.

With variable annuity products you have the availability of sub-accounts from some of the best money managers in the world. In addition to that variety, you often have asset allocation models, and the availability of the major market indexes. These sub-accounts are all reviewed and monitored for performance against their peers by the investment managers at the insurance companies. The performance history on many of these products is quite impressive.

Now that you are beginning to understand what annuities are and why you should consider them, the next question is when an annuity should be employed.

Annuities are Only a Piece of Your Financial Plan

First, annuities should be considered only as part of a comprehensive financial plan. They are not a one-size-fits-all product. Be wary of the advisor who only sells annuities, or favors them too much. If the only tool you have is a hammer, every problem you have looks like a nail! Often when annuities have received bad press, it is because too much of a client's assets have been positioned in them.

Annuities are appropriate when you no longer have a need or an appetite for risk within a portion of your portfolio. They also should be considered when other tax-sheltered savings such as IRAs or 401ks have been maximized.

Deferred annuities should only be considered for portions of your assets that will be invested for a longer time horizon. They are not a short-term investment. (top chart)

Immediate annuities are a time-tested way to provide tax-efficient income that is guaranteed to last as long as you do. Guarantees like this — especially as we continue to live longer — are powerful. The bottom chart on the following page demonstrates how soon $100,000 can be spent if it is not

Here's How a Deferred Annuity Works:

Makes Premium Payments During Accumulation Phase

| Annuitant | | Insurance Company |

2
Pays a Lifetime Income During Payout Phase

3
Pays Any Survivor Benefits

| Beneficiary |

1. During the accumulation phase prior to retirement, the annuitant makes a single or periodic annuity premium payments to an insurance company.

2. At retirement, the annuitant selects an annuity payout option and the insurance company pays the annuitant a guaranteed* income for as long as the annuitant is alive. The portion of each annuity payment representing earnings on annuity premiums is subject to income tax as received.

3. If the annuitant dies during the accumulation phase, the insurance company pays the accumulated value of the tax-deferred annuity to the annuitant's designated beneficiary. If the annuitant dies during the payout phase, there may be survivor benefits payable to the annuitant's designated beneficiary, depending on the annuity payout option selected.

* Guarantee is based on the continued claims-paying ability of the insurer.

How Long Will Your Retirement Savings Last?

If You Withdraw Both Principal and Interest,
How Long Will It Take to Exhaust a
$100,000 Retirement Savings Fund?

Rate of Return	Amount Withdrawn at the Beginning of Each Month:		
	$1,000	$2,000	$3,000
4%	121 monthly payments (10 years, 1 month)	54 monthly payments (4 years, 6 months)	35 monthly payments (2 years, 11 months)
6%	138 monthly payments (11 years, 6 months)	57 monthly payments (4 years, 9 months)	36 monthly payments (3 years)
8%	165 monthly payments (13 years, 9 months)	61 monthly payments (5 years, 1 month)	37 monthly payments (3 years, 1 month)
10%	215 monthly payments (17 years, 11 months)	64 monthly payments (5 years, 4 months)	39 monthly payments (3 years, 3 months)

If we knew exactly how long we were going to live after retirement, this arrangement might be satisfactory. The reality, of course, is that none of us knows how long we will live after retirement. This uncertainty is what makes it so difficult to avoid the risk of outliving retirement income.

protected by an annuity. Knowing you can't outlive your income provides great peace of mind.

What to do Next?

If you're still with me and are considering learning more about the specifics of annuities, you will have to decide how and where to buy them. Everyone from your banker to your broker to the fellow who used to work with you who has suddenly become a "financial advisor," is selling annuities. Although I will admit a personal bias, I strongly recommend you work with a credentialed advisor with several years of quality industry experience who also offers other products and solutions.

There are numerous professional designations and seemingly more popping up each day, however a few are most credible and recognized: Certified Financial Planner™ (CFP®), Chartered Life Underwriter (CLU), Chartered Financial Consultant (ChFC), Certified Senior Advisor (CSA), or Life Underwriter Training Council Fellow (LUTCF). Although they differ in their credentialing process and focus, all require comprehensive exams, continuing education programs, ethics requirements, and a client-centered approach. You can learn more about these designations and local holders of them by using your favorite search tool on the Internet or check the website http://www.wiseadvisor.com/designations.asp.

Once you begin working with an advisor and are considering specific annuity products, solid financial ratings are very important. AM Best Company rates a company's ability to meet ongoing obligations to its policyholders. You should focus on companies that have an A or better rating from AM Best. Some smaller regional companies may not meet these standards, but this does not mean they don't have good products. However, you should be very careful, and only use these carriers if they have exceptional policy provisions that you can't find with an A-rated carrier. Standard and Poor's and Fitch Ratings can also be considered when researching the appropriate company.

It's a good idea to ask for performance history
on the products you are interested in.
Although the past is not a predictor of
the future, seeing how a product actually
performed will help you to better
understand how it may perform for you.

Next, you need to accurately compare the contract provisions, which are described earlier in this chapter. Be sure you understand surrender charges, expense charges, contract guarantees, withdrawal provisions and any other riders or nuances of the proposed contract. I suggest that you work with an advisor who can present several products from different carriers; this will help you to choose a product that best meets your needs. Remember the hammer story!

It's a good idea to ask for performance history on the products you are interested in. Although the past is not a predictor of the future, seeing how a product actually performed will help you to better understand how it may perform for you. Don't be afraid to ask questions (understanding that even the sharpest advisor may not have every answer); however, he or she should be able to get the answer.

Earlier we covered exchange from existing annuities. This often, but certainly not always, makes sense. State regulations vary widely, but most require a replacement comparison before the exchange takes place. Be sure you understand the downside on these transactions as well as the potential improvements. The major areas to focus on are any existing surrender charges on your current annuity, new surrender charge periods for the new contract, changes in death benefit and ongoing expense charges. Refer back to the earlier part in this chapter and compare the pertinent policy provisions.

The Last Word

We have discussed the importance of the advisor's credibility and knowledge, and the need to work with a quality company with sound financial ratings and a good, solid performance history. You have an important role to play, also. Be sure to let your advisor know the whole truth about all of your needs and goals and disclose to that individual all of your assets and income, even if you do not plan on investing those assets with the new advisor. The appropriateness of annuities within your plan depends on complete and accurate information and risk assessment. The more forthcoming you are, the better your plan will serve you.

If you are nearing or in retirement, your most important priorities should be preservation and distribution planning. Annuities can play a major part in helping you achieve your goals in this challenging, yet exciting, endeavor.

When people ask me what I do for a living I explain to them that I help people keep promises — Promises they have made to themselves, their family and their community. If one of the promises you have made to yourself is that you will not outlive your assets during retirement, annuities can help you keep that promise.

◆◆◆

 **Arnie Pechler III**, CFP®, CSA, LUTCF, LLIF, MBA, has been involved with the insurance and financial services industry since 1977. He is multi-state licensed for life and health insurance, holds a property and casualty license and is a NASD registered representative.

Arnie is a Certified Financial Planner™, Certified Senior Advisor, Life Underwriter Training Council Fellow, Limra Leadership Institue Fellow and holds an MBA degree.

He has been an agent, general agent, and home office senior executive during his career. Arnie has returned to his upstate New York roots, living in Macedon, N.Y. where he is a member of Rotary and involved with several community and civic organizations. Arnie is a regular newspaper columnist and is a frequent speaker and writer on both financial and personal development topics.

Arnie can be reached at United Professional Advisors, 1025 Brixton Drive, Suite 1, Macedon, New York 14502; (tel) 315.986.3765; (email) apechler@tarkentonfinancial.com.

An Estate Plan
Of Significance
For Multi-Generations

Larry L. Van Oort, President
Family Legacy Planning Specialists

"This is mankind's age-old
dilemma in the face of death:
what man really fears is not so
much extinction, but extinction with
insignificance. Man wants to know
that his life has somehow counted,
that it has left a trace, a trace that
has meaning; its effects must
remain alive in eternity some way."

– Ernest Becker –
Pulitzer Prize-Winning Author

A significant life, then, is one that has meaning. What does meaning mean? It means, *"to stand for, to represent."* A significant life, however, stands for much more than something tangible or literal, such as someone's life span and accumulated financial assets. A significant life is a full, quality life because it stands not only for principles that find their core in the foundation of our humanness, but also because these principles are passed on and revered, are communicated and become permanent.

What are such principles? How about duty, honor, country? Or, family, faith, and charity? Or, spirituality, excellence, and empathy? What about yours?

While more and more people are living longer and some are accumulating more and more financial assets, anecdotally speaking, there are fewer and fewer people whose principled lives are being communicated to and revered by their descendents. Why?

Here are two related reasons:

1. Traditional planning, a science, which includes technical asset management, retirement planning, estate and tax planning, are not seeming to consistently, humanly *connect* the two, three, or even four generations being planned for by clients' traditional advisory team. Goals for traditional planning typically include that the spouses will care for each other while both are alive, that the survivor will be financially okay, that every nickel will later go to the kids, and that estate taxes will be avoided or minimized. Few principles here. Where is the family *connection?*

2. Dysfunctional social relationships between family members appear on the increase. *"Ninety percent of the problems in inheritance can be avoided by talking to your parents before they die."* —John L. Levy, Psychological Consultant Specialist in the *Problems of Inheritors*.

Also increasing is their dysfunctional relationship with their financial wealth. Stories about the negative effects of receiving unearned financial wealth are not infrequent. *"By the end of the third generation, 90 percent of wealthy families will have lost the family wealth."* —E. G. Link, Family Wealth Counseling.

Traditional planning, to be clear, is essential for making sure technical, scientific procedures are carefully designed and executed. However, it can sometimes seem dry or intimidating to the people it is intended to help and protect. Some of them do not genuinely *connect with it emotionally, do not connect it to their hearts.* Furthermore, because traditional planning's many complicated aspects can require special consultants, the clients' advisory team members are not always well-known to the family's succeeding generations or even to the other advisory team members.

Some people's difficulty with convergently meshing the art of their emotional planning with the science of their traditional planning can be evident in their intra-family relationships.

Some people's difficulty with convergently meshing the art of their emotional planning with the science of their traditional planning can be evident in their intra-family relationships. For a number of reasons, such as social mobility, employment opportunities, and different cultural tastes, immediate and extended family members are becoming more divergent in their relationships and are having fewer and fewer direct social connections. The annual family reunions are seldom annual. Sunday dinners among families seem rarer and rarer.

Only a major holiday or two, along with a funeral or a wedding, seem to bring families together. Whenever they do meet, the length and quality of time together, however, can be brief and shallow. Is it any wonder that when financial wealth is transferred pre- or post-mortem, those receiving it are more and more often perceived as being less and less appreciative. *"How long does the average recipient of an inheritance wait before they buy a new car? Just nineteen days."* —New Car Dealer Association

So, what is the solution for fewer principled lives not being understood and respected by their descendents? It is spanning the generations' emotional void with meaningful human connections so the science of traditional planning fuses with the art of the family's foundational principles. Spanning families' generational voids undergirds their mutual significance.

How to do this? By recognizing fundamental failures within some families and then implementing the steps required for rectifying those failures. Within this context, one must understand that the definition of family is multi-generational; that is, there are typically first, second, third, and, sometimes, fourth generations involved. With this understood, here are the major failures in sequential order:

1. Have not orally discussed, discovered, and audio-recorded family values, visions, and general financial objectives.

2. Have not distilled those values, visions, and general financial objectives into an organized, written document for permanency and communication.

3. Have not worked with the family's team of professional advisors in a coordinated fashion so advancement of the family's agenda could be the focus of the team's strategic and tactical expertise.

4. Have not established a family business/governmental body for formally structuring activities, focusing family energies, and mutually mentoring to one another for the advancement of the family's values, visions, and general financial objectives.

To explain and illustrate how significance-seeking families can recognize and rectify their fundamental failures, let me tell you a true story about a man I'll call Bill.

Usually, the generation most concerned with significance is the first, or oldest generation. They determine that they want to leave a trace of *themselves,* not just their financial assets. So it was with Bill, who was in his early 60s and more than 15 years into his third marriage, when his "significance-seeking light" went on. He was increasingly concerned that, while his financial picture was becoming brighter, the picture of his relationship with his three adult children and three grandchildren was dim with little prospect of getting brighter. In fact, if he had any more disagreements with his children during his awkward, stilted meetings with them, he feared the light would go out completely.

Guided Discovery™[1]

Guided by another person, Bill was asked a series of opened-ended questions beginning with his early years. Here is a sampling: "Tell us about the home and family you grew up in." Or, "While growing up, what characteristics about your father did you most admire?" "What do you think are the strongest three attributes of your mother?" "How do you try to live by your parents' characteristics and attributes?"

Some questions about his middle years were, "Give the history of your relationship with your business partner." "When you think about him, what comes to mind?" "How are your personal goals the same as your business partner's?" "What is the significance of that?"

Regarding his current family relationships, Bill was asked, "When you think about family, what comes to mind?" "How are your goals your children's goals?" "Regarding your children, state each one's strongest attribute?" "In what areas would you like each of them to improve?" "What is important about that to you?"

Turning to Bill's visions for the future, he was asked, "Five years from now, what would you like the picture of your relationship with your three children and grandchildren to look like?" "Fifteen years from now?" "What do your children really know about your story?" "If you could give them something other than money, what would that be? Why?"

By carefully reading the transcript of his nearly eight hours of conversation, Bill was able to infer what his values and visions were along with

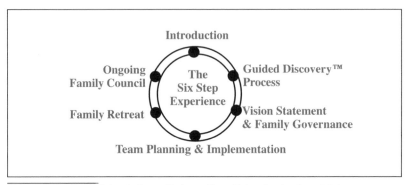

---

[1] A process developed by The Heritage Institute, and implemented by certified members, http://www.theheritagecenter.com.

framing where his general financial objectives should be directed. Here is his distillation of what was most important to him:

1. He wanted a second chance at being a parent and a grandparent because being in a loving, mutually respectful relationship with his children was clearly what he wanted most.

2. He wanted his children and grandchildren involved in his business dealings during his life so they would be prepared after his death.

3. He wanted his three children to really know, love, and trust one another because he knew they currently did not.

Bill then wrote down his discovery. As a result, all became permanent: his stories and the events that influenced him, the values he derived from them, his visions for the future relationships he wanted, and his general financial objectives so his financial wealth would support his family (emotional) wealth.

His discovery, and making it permanent, was the good news. The bad news was that Bill did not know what his children wanted or how to communicate with them about his discovery and its potential significance. How could he tell them, given their history of awkward, stilted discussions that seldom ended without him feeling disconnected and alone?

The answer: Each of them should also experience Guided Discovery™. Which they did.

Since Bill's financial affairs were as orderly as he could get them given his relationship with his three children, there was little more to do regarding working with his team of trusted, technical advisors other than give them each a copy of his written document. This way, they would all be, for the first time, sharing the same information about their common client, Bill. How often does this happen?

Then, this disconnected family of four met on a Saturday morning at Bill's beautiful new home. (Each of the children lived in rented apartments which were not in the best parts of town.) All members came with their written documents in hand. After stiffly seating themselves in a circle in the family room, Bill began reading his document aloud to the others; then, in descending chronological order, the children read theirs aloud.

When the circle was completed, a feeling comparable to the sensation of having a painful abscessed tooth extracted permeated them. While each family member was temporarily numb, all began sensing feelings within themselves that they had not felt since they could remember. Joy began welling up from each member's soul just as tears welled up in their eyes. After countless years of separation, simultaneously they realized they had just *connected* as a family. Missing family feelings returned. Why? Because they all learned they wanted the same things: a second chance at being a family, the opportunity to mutually mentor each other, the opportunity to grow together, no longer apart.

After assessing their strengths during their afternoon meeting, they elected officers, adopted a charter and by-laws previously drafted by Bill. Then, Bill announced that he had deposited $100,000 into their family bank as a tool so they could learn how money works.

Since then, they meet at least monthly. They have learned about investments, taxes, accounting, and real estate for a start. Most importantly, they have learned about each other's values, agendas, and dreams. By having the structure for permitting them to be open and honest without concern for judgment, their emotional growth is taking them from fearful children to self-actualized adults.

TRUTH
by James Hearst

HOW THE devil do I know
if there are rocks in your field,
plow it and find out.
If the plow strikes something
harder than earth, the point
shatters at a sudden blow
and the tractor jerks sidewise
and dumps you off the seat–
because the spring hitch
isn't set to trip quickly enough
and it never is–probably
you hit a rock. That means
the glacier emptied his pocket
in your field as well as mine,
but the CONNECTION with a thing
is the only truth that I know of,
so plow it.

So, two major causes of family disconnection are (1) planning that does not genuinely connect generations and (2) dysfunctional relationships among family members themselves and their receipt of unearned wealth. However, as Bill's story illustrates, it does not have to be this way. Families can considerably mitigate, if not eliminate, these causes. While there are no guarantees, by fusing the science of traditional planning with the art employed by Bill's family, clients who want to achieve significance in their lives have the means. The only essential missing now is the personal commitment to do so. Commitment, however, is the grist of another chapter.

"There are seven things that will destroy us:
Wealth without work; Pleasure without
conscience; Knowledge without character;
Religion without sacrifice; Politics without
principle; Science without humanity;
Business without ethics."

— Mohandas K. Gandhi

◆◆◆

Larry L. Van Oort, CWC™, CFP®, President, Family Legacy Planning Specialists™, earned his BA & MA in English along with a Russian minor from the University of Northern Iowa. Larry spent 15 years as a successful English teacher and football coach at the high school and community college levels. Seeking new challenges, he then entered the world of financial planning in the late 1980s. He steadily grew his own privately-held practice. During this time he also earned his Certified Financial Planner® designation and his Certified Wealth Consultant designation. He held offices in his area chapter of Financial Planning Association.

Three years ago Larry expanded his vision to specialize in family legacy planning, which means connecting clients' financial wealth (tangible) with their family wealth (intangible) for the purpose of clients' achieving personal significance. Seeking the expertise to restore the missing balance between these two assets, Larry became a member of The Heritage Institute (www.theheritageinstitute.com) and acquired the specialized expertise of their designation, Certified Wealth Consultant, and formed Family Legacy Planning Specialists™.

Today, he travels the country helping significance-seeking clients discover their important insights and understandings including the people and events that instilled them. Once discovered, they are distilled into written documents and disseminated to people and organizations important to them. To learn more about Larry and his specialty, see www.lvanoort.com. Larry can be reached at Family Legacy Planning Specialists, P.O. Box 201, Cedar Falls, Iowa 50613; (tel) 319.277.1489; (email) private@lvanoort.com.

Estate Planning:
Maximizing the Potential

Chuck KinCannon, J.D., LL.M.
Attorney and Counselor at Law

In writing this chapter on estate planning, I faced a dilemma: trying to determine the true definition of estate planning.

- Is estate planning a transaction that produces documents, or

- Is estate planning a values-based process that is reflected in the form of documents?

In either case, a client and the advisors need to determine exactly what they mean by "estate planning."

From my experience, every client needs to first define what estate planning means to them. Many of my clients have adopted the following as a good traditional definition of estate planning:

"I want to control my property while I am alive, take care of myself and my loved ones if I become disabled, give what I have, to whom I want, when I want, and the way I want. And, if I can, I would like to save every court cost, tax dollar and professional fee possible while protecting myself and my loved ones from creditors and predators."

To illustrate how to accomplish this, let's examine a traditional family and the challenges they might face in estate planning:

Richard and Mary are 60 and 56 years old respectively. They have been married 35 years and have two children, Bob and Sue. Bob is 30 years old and a plastic surgeon. Sue is 25 with two children, one of whom has a disability. Richard and Mary have a combined estate of $3.5 million including $500,000 of life insurance, and $500,000 in IRAs. Both Richard and Mary like the definition of estate planning described on the previous page and would like to accomplish each objective in the definition. They are particularly concerned about their son Bob who is a physician exposed to lawsuits and a spendthrift. They are also concerned about their granddaughter who has special needs due to her disability.

After discussing their goals, Richard and Mary need to understand the two approaches to estate planning. One approach uses wills as the primary instrument of the estate plan. Wills are a dispositive instrument giving instructions for how the estate should be distributed at death. Wills must be probated prior to the property being distributed.

Trusts, on the other hand, are instruments that contain instructions for how the client's assets (also known as the estate) are to be managed during Richard and Mary's lifetime as well as how they are to be managed and distributed at Richard and Mary's death.

Trusts are created by the client (often referred to as a grantor, settlor or trustmaker), and are managed by one or more trustees. Trusts can be revocable or irrevocable. Revocable trusts are often used as the main estate planning tool with irrevocable trusts established to accomplish specific objectives such as estate tax planning and asset protection.

Since a will only addresses how the property
will be distributed at death, additional
documents are needed to address
the needs and concerns of disability.

Since a will only addresses how the property will be distributed at death, additional documents are needed to address the needs and concerns of disability. General durable powers of attorney for property and finances would be used by Richard and Mary to name an agent to exercise legal authority on their behalf just as if they each were doing an action themselves. In most cases, the powers of attorney take effect immediately. Typically, the powers are general and broad and, if drafted properly, will survive disability (or be "durable"). Since most powers of attorney are standardized and broad, they may give the agent either too little authority or too much authority.

In addition, there is ongoing evidence that these documents will not be accepted by financial institutions that want to restrict the authority of the agent and limit the liability of the institution. For this reason, if a will-based plan is used with a general durable power of attorney, it is recommended that Richard and Mary obtain a special limited power of attorney from all institutions where they have accounts.

A trust-based plan reduces the need to rely on these types of powers of attorney because the trust will designate a disability trustee to manage all property titled in the name of the trust. In addition, a properly drafted trust will reflect the exact circumstances when the disability trustee will assume his or her role and what powers the disability trustee will have over the assets of the trust. Even with a trust, however, limited powers of attorney are needed for transferring assets to the trust by the agent if the grantor becomes disabled and for handling any financial matters which are not directly related to the trust itself. The most common situation deals with the management of accounts such as IRAs since the title to the IRA must remain with the individual. Beneficiary issues will be discussed in a later part of this chapter.

After considering the benefits and attributes of each type of plan, Richard and Mary have decided to use a trust-based plan to avoid the necessity of relying exclusively on general powers of attorney. As discussed above, however, they will still need to use limited powers of attorney to cover situations such as management of their IRAs, filing tax returns and other financial issues.

Since disability is statistically far more likely to occur than death, it is crucial that all healthcare-related documents be drafted.

In addition to financial issues, there are other important matters that must be addressed by Richard and Mary. It is very important for them to have healthcare agents designated using what is usually referred to as a durable power of attorney for healthcare authorized by statute in most states. In this document, Richard and Mary would name healthcare agents who would have the authority to make decisions for them as well as carry our their instructions for decisions such as life support. Since disability is statistically far more likely to occur than death, it is crucial that all healthcare-related documents be drafted to not only comply with state law, but also to reflect the most personal wishes and preferences of Richard and Mary. Along with the healthcare powers of attorney, most states also authorize the use of a living will or declaration to physicians. These documents state the type of treatment Richard and Mary may or may not want. Between the two documents, however, the durable power of attorney for healthcare is usually more important and enforceable since physicians may or may not uphold the wishes in a living will.

More recently, there have been issues where the healthcare or financial agent have been unable to obtain medical records needed to make decisions in their respective roles. This has occurred mainly due to a federal law called HIPAA (Health Insurance Portability and Accountability Act) which makes it difficult for someone other than the patient to obtain his or her medical records. For that reason, Richard and Mary would need a HIPAA authorization form which would appoint a HIPAA agent for them. These agents are usually the same individuals named to serve in other capacities for Richard and Mary,

One problem that Richard and Mary may face is the inability for them or their agents to locate the healthcare documents when they are needed. To solve this problem, there are companies such as Docubank that will electronically store copies of all executed healthcare documents. By doing this, Richard and Mary and their agents will have continuous access to these documents anytime and anywhere they may be.

Thus far, we have examined disability planning in an estate plan. We have compared the use of a will-based plan with a trust-based plan. At this point, it might be good to pause and look at some obstacles that would prevent either or both plans from working effectively for Richard and Mary.

Potential Estate Planning Obstacles

From my experience, the single most prevalent reason why estate plans do not work effectively is related to how assets are titled and beneficiaries are designated. Most individuals are told to own assets jointly with their spouse if they are married. They are also told to name the spouse as beneficiary of all life insurance and retirement plans such as IRAs. This was how Richard and Mary's titles and beneficiaries were structured prior to their planning.

The potential problems with this are many. First, any assets owned jointly with rights of survivorship or assets with beneficiary designations will not pass through the estate plan (will or trust) unless the estate or trust is named as beneficiary. The assets will pass to the other joint tenant or the beneficiary, as the case may be.

It is absolutely crucial to know how each and every asset in [your] estate is titled in order to know who will ultimately control or own each asset.

If this occurs, Richard and Mary will forfeit control of their assets and not be able to attach any instructions for how the assets should be used. This is particularly important when a goal is to place restrictions on the use of the assets or when there is a taxable estate. In Richard and Mary's case, they have both. Thus, it is absolutely crucial to know how each and every asset in their estate is titled in order to know who will ultimately control or own each asset.

In the case of a trust-based estate plan, it is even more crucial to ensure that the trust own as many of the assets as legally allowed so that the instructions of the trust will apply to the use and management and, ultimately, the distribution of those assets. To further ensure the effectiveness of an estate plan and to maximize income tax savings as well as estate tax savings, it is also very important to properly integrate any IRAs, 401(k)s or other retirement plans into the estate plan since these assets have special rules that apply to them. These rules can often create loss of control and unnecessary taxes to individuals and their advisors who do not understand the intricacies of such planning. In Richard and Mary's case, it is very important for proper integration since they not only have a taxable estate but they also want to exert control over the IRAs just as they do the rest of their estate. There are a number of options available to do this including establishing separate IRA trusts. A complete discussion of these options is beyond the scope of this chapter, but this issue should not be overlooked in doing proper estate planning. It is crucial that a knowledgeable financial advisor and estate planning attorney be consulted.

So, now we have examined disability issues and funding or titling of assets. If both of these issues are properly addressed, Richard and Mary will have an excellent probability of maintaining control of their assets and having their personal wishes followed in the event of disability.

What to do in the Event of a Death

The next event that normally occurs in an estate plan is the death of the first spouse.

This event creates several issues that should be addressed. In Richard and Mary's case, they need to be concerned about preserving any estate tax exemptions and exclusions they may have under federal and state law. To do this, two things must occur. First, the assets must be titled properly so that neither Richard nor Mary have more than the amount of one of their exemptions in their name and trust. Second, the estate plan must contain tax planning, most commonly in the form of a credit shelter or bypass trust.

This trust would be created at the death of the first spouse, primarily to preserve the estate tax exemption of the first spouse. Unfortunately, even plans that do contain this type of planning often do so with boilerplate provisions that not only overlook important client considerations, but also actually cause unnecessary income tax. (A discussion of funding formulas is beyond the scope of this chapter but one should be aware of this issue if there is a taxable estate, and should consult a knowledgeable estate planning attorney who is trained to deal with these issues).

It is just as important to customize this bypass trust as it is to customize the overall plan to meet Richard and Mary's objectives. In their case, they wanted to not only preserve the estate tax exemptions, but they also wanted to provide planning in the event the surviving spouse remarries. Their trust-based plan should be drafted to reflect these objectives. In today's society, remarriage is very common and can create a stressful, if not disastrous, set of consequences for the estate plan and its effects on the heirs. In addition, selection of trustees, disability planning for the surviving spouse, and other specific issues exist during this time period.

At the second death, the estate plan matures for the benefit of the children. As mentioned at the beginning of the chapter, Richard and Mary have two children (Sue and Bob), each with unique abilities and weaknesses. In planning for Bob, it is important to focus on how to leave his inheritance to him. He not only has exposure to creditors, but he also has a tendency to spend money freely. Richard and Mary are concerned about both. In Bob's particular situation, Richard and Mary opted to create an asset protection trust for Bob's benefit with a third party independent trustee managing the assets. Since Bob is both financially successful and a spendthrift, Richard and Mary would prefer to allow him to access the trust for true needs rather than have total access to the funds. By doing so, the trust funds will be available for Bob when he really needs them. In addition, if Bob's trust is structured properly, it can also be protected from his creditors and from his spouse in the event of a divorce. Protecting inherited assets from creditors has become very important in many estate plans.

Sue, on the other hand, has different issues. Although she is not a very good money manager, she is frugal. Richard and Mary have less concern about Sue's access to the funds than they do about providing for her and her disabled daughter.

Richard and Mary could establish a special needs trust for the benefit of their disabled granddaughter, but they elected to leave Sue's share in trust for the benefit of Sue.

They need to look beyond Sue, however, to ensure that Sue's daughter will never receive any funds outright because, if she did, Sue's daughter may become disqualified to receive any assistance for her disability.

Other Issues

Richard and Mary's situation seems pretty basic. From this basic situation, however, it should be apparent that there really is nothing basic about it. The complexity of the laws governing specific assets such as IRAs, titles and beneficiaries when combined with numerous individual personal objectives make any plan a challenge. Each and every situation is unique and should be approached as such.

In traditional planning, there are many other vehicles available beyond the basic planning tools of the will-based plan or the trust-based plan. These vehicles include establishing asset protection trusts, limited liability companies, corporations, irrevocable trusts for estate tax reduction and/or creditor protection and various types of charitable vehicles.

In Richard and Mary's situation, a comprehensive plan using basic tools that are highly customized meet their overall planning objectives. In addition, as already mentioned, Richard may elect to establish an IRA trust for his IRA in order to control the distributions from his IRA. This may be particularly important because of their disabled grandchild.

At this point, Richard and Mary have a very solid plan, traditionally speaking. Why do I say traditionally? Because if all Richard and Mary do is look at the structure without looking at the meaning behind the structure, their plan may not really fulfill their true intentions. In addition, most estate plans, even if they include all of the provisions we have discussed so far, do very little to prepare the heirs for their inheritance.

> Preparing the heirs for the inheritance is just as necessary as preparing a comprehensive plan to transfer the assets.

For that reason, it is very important for Richard and Mary to discuss practical methods of not only getting their *valuables* to their children, but also their *values* that allowed them to create their estate. There are several ways of doing this, some of which are discussed in Chapter 8 of this book. In my opinion, anyone who has an estate of any significant value and who truly cares about his or her family should examine this as part of their overall estate planning. Preparing the heirs for the inheritance is just as necessary as preparing a comprehensive plan to transfer the assets.

Conclusion

In conclusion, there are numerous risks in, and consequences of, not doing proper estate planning. Some of these occur during lifetime and others after death. They range from loss of control, taxes and distribution issues to inadequate preparation of the heirs to receive the inheritance.

On the other hand, there are abundant opportunities to not only avoid the most aggravating obstacles and issues, but also to pass values along with valuables to those people and causes one cares about. Richard and Mary were able to do just that by investing the time in considering their many options and working with a qualified estate planning attorney. Your story can also have a happy ending. The choice is yours.

◆◆◆

Chuck KinCannon brings more than 20 years of experience as a domestic and international attorney, consulting and advising individuals and business owners. His diverse multi-cultural and international experiences allow him to provide a unique perspective as an attorney and wealth consultant certified by The Heritage Institute. With this experience, he is prepared to empower his clients to protect what matters most to them: the assets they have worked hard to accumulate, the values and significance making their success possible, and the ability to help them transfer both to the people and organizations they care about most.

Chuck received his B.A. with high honors from the University of Denver. He went on to receive his Juris Doctorate from Southern Methodist University School of Law and his Master of Laws from Columbia University School of Law where he was appointed an international fellow and served as associate editor of the *Columbia Business Law Review*. Chuck has been a contributing author of several books on business and estate planning, and has taught hundreds of seminars to lay and professional audiences.

Chuck is a member of the state bars of Georgia, Florida, and Texas, and is a Fellow with the College of the State Bar of Texas. In addition, he is admitted to practice in the United States Tax Court.

Chuck KinCannon can be reached at: 1870 The Exchange, Ste 100, Atlanta, GA 30339; (tel) 770-951-7033; (email) chuck@us-law.net.

The Generosity Revolution:
Planning to Make a Difference

Steven M. Lear, ChFC, CLU, President
Affiance Financial, LLC

"We are not generous because
we are rich. We are rich
because we are generous."

— Claire L. Gaudiani, activist
Author of *The Greater Good*

By now, almost everyone is aware of the remarkable philanthropic merger of Warren Buffet and the Bill and Melinda Gates Foundation. Buffet recently made a monumental decision: rather than waiting to distribute his enormous wealth to charitable causes upon his death, he would begin the process now, at age 75. Even more astounding is rather than setting up his own foundation, he will donate 85 percent of his Berkshire Hathaway stock (currently valued at well over $40 billion) to five established foundations. Four-fifths of this distribution will go to the $30 billion Bill and Melinda Gates Foundation, creating a charitable organization of nearly $60 billion. Assuming an annual distribution rate of five percent, this foundation could produce $3 billion annually to help solve some of the world's problems. Imagine the possibilities.

To those of us who are charitable minded, it's easy to be intimidated by such daunting figures. But don't be fooled into thinking that you can't play an integral role in helping solve the world's problems by making your own commitments to causes you support. In both my personal and professional life,

I have been inspired countless times by ordinary individuals making extraordinary contributions to the world.

I'm reminded of Abe, a 75-year-old widower with a modest net worth, who became a client of mine 13 years ago. I helped him put together a financial plan and we set up a system to create a monthly income for him. (I also fixed him up with my mother, whom he dated until his death this past year, but that's another story.) Abe was a kind and caring man, and during one of our meetings, I asked him if he planned to leave his entire net worth to his children. We discussed the idea of using a small portion of his net worth to establish a family foundation. He expressed an interest in leaving some portion of his wealth to his community, and he especially liked the idea of his children working together after his death to distribute the income from the foundation to charitable causes.

Shortly after Abe's death last year, his three children came to my office to review his financial papers. Among his papers, we came across the annuity contract that funded his IRA; a donor-advised fund was named as the beneficiary of this contract. As I recounted my conversations with Abe to his children, and told them about his vision for them to one day work together to distribute the foundation's income, their eyes welled up with tears. "My dad was the greatest," his son said.

Clearly, Abe's children were deeply moved not only by their father's quiet generosity, but also by his greater desire to give future generations of his family an opportunity to participate together in this act of charity. It will be interesting to see how this relatively small family foundation will propagate, helping those in need and binding together future generations of Abe's family in meaningful ways for years to come.

Charity Begins at Home

There is plenty of anti-American sentiment these days from the international community. Among other things, Americans are often accused of being materialistic, opulent, even stingy. Interesting accusation, in light of the overwhelming evidence that the United States is among the most generous nations in the history of the world, consider these facts:

- The American people give approximately $3 billion to charity every 4½ days.[1]
- The total amount of charitable giving in 2004 was $249 billion–almost $260.28 billion in 2005.
- 89% of Americans contribute to charitable causes.
- 55% of Americans volunteer their time to a charitable cause.
- Total giving has increased in 41 out of the last 42 years.

---

[1] Meyerson, In Character magazine. http://www.nptrust.org/philanthropy/philanthropy_stats.asp

- It is estimated that between 6.6 trillion to 27.4 trillion in charitable bequests will be made between 1998 and 2052.
- There are approximately 1,010,400 charitable organizations in the United States, with an additional 355,000 religious congregations.
- The non-profit sector employs 10.2 million people, accounting for 6.9% of the total U.S. work force.

"Giving is a by-product of living in a free society, where individuals truly have the power and opportunity to make a difference."

— Adam Meyerson, President, Philanthropy Roundtable

According to Adam Meyerson, president of the Philanthropy Roundtable, in an interview with *In Character* magazine, "America is off the charts in how charitable we are compared with other countries, and this has been true from the very beginning of our history." Citing reasons for our national tendency towards generosity, Meyerson points first and foremost to our high rate of religious affiliation. Those who regularly attend weekly religious services give three times as much of their income than those who are not regular attendees, and they tend to give across the board, not just to their religious organizations. In addition, Meyerson notes that our giving is a by-product of living in a free society, where individuals truly have the power and opportunity to make a difference.

Charitably speaking, there is more we could, and *should*, be doing. Currently, charitable giving accounts for 2.1% of the gross domestic product, and this figure has remained level since the depression. To increase this number, Meyerson suggests "capturing the charitable imagination of the American people."

The Zero-Estate-Tax Plan: How to Leave a Legacy

I was introduced to one idea that I had never imagined almost 20 years ago at the annual conference of the Million Dollar Round Table (MDRT), a premier organization of life insurance and financial services providers. Among the speakers at that meeting was Ron Philgreen, a noted expert in charitable estate planning. He spoke about the "Zero Estate Tax Plan," which made so much sense that my wife and I decided to implement it in our family. Using this plan, we decided on an appropriate amount of money to leave to our children. Our goal was to leave them a financial legacy that would provide them with a "safety net" without diminishing their ambition to strive for success on their own. In other words, we wanted to *protect* them from extreme hardship without *enabling* them. We then purchased a life insurance policy that would assure this financial legacy to our children. Since life insurance proceeds come in the form of a check, the money will be easily divisible and distributable upon our deaths. Having comfortably satisfied our legacy to our children, all other assets that we accumulate in our lifetime will now flow first to the surviving spouse, and then to a *family foundation*. All of these assets will flow to the foundation income and estate tax-free.

There are a few important decisions to make when establishing a family foundation:

- Decide which charitable entities will receive the gifts. One option is for donors (in this case, my wife and me) to choose the organizations that will receive distributions. Another option is for the donors to specify the fields of interest (for example: healthcare, education, or a particular religious community) and then allow the foundation advisors (in this case, our children) to choose the specific organizations within those categories. Some donors set up their foundation by giving the named advisors full discretion as to where to allocate the funds.

- Determine an annual distributable amount to allocate to charitable organizations each year. This can either be in the form of a set annual dollar amount, or a percentage of the balance of the fund as of a specified date each year. I recommend the latter of these options.

- Select an organization to act as a philanthropic agent or create a private foundation; the agent can be a community foundation or other donor-advised funds. We used the American Endowment Foundation based in Ohio. Creating a private foundation is much more complicated; I recommend that you speak to your accountant and attorney if you choose to set up your own foundation.

The final step in our process was to write a philanthropic will, in which we imparted to our children the importance of this family foundation, and expressed our hopes that they will work together to distribute the earnings to worthy organizations after our deaths. While the philanthropic will is non-binding in the legal sense, it is as worthy a document as any to include in one's estate planning documents. (To learn more about philanthropic wills, please go to http://www.philanthropicwill.com.)

Implementing the Zero Estate Tax Plan has turned out to be a most liberating experience. The combination of purchasing the insurance and establishing the foundation has made us feel confident that we have provided for our children and our community. *An unexpected benefit of this plan is that it gives us the freedom to spend our cash flow as we wish.* For me, this means becoming more active in what I refer to as the "Generosity Revolution."

The Generosity Revolution Emerges:
Time to Get on the Bandwagon

The Generosity Revolution, as I see it, emerged following the tragic events of September 11, 2001. According to the Corporation for National and Community Service, Americans increased their volunteerism significantly since 9/11. In 2002, 59.7 million Americans claimed to volunteer their time; that number rose to 65.4 million in 2005. Perhaps prompted by 9/11, and further motivated to help after Hurricanes Katrina and Rita, it appears that Americans are learning they are equally motivated by psychic income as much as monetary, or tangible income. Monetary income is crucial; it allows you to pay bills, buy and maintain a home, accumulate assets, travel, etc. Psychic income, on the other hand, nurtures the mind and soul. It is the payment you receive from your non-employment activities: raising a family, participating in a favorite sport or hobby, traveling, volunteering, etc. Other than raising a family, I would argue that volunteering provides the greatest amount of psychic income. Think of what we could accomplish in the world if people earned more of their psychic income through volunteering!

So, how does one hop on the generosity bandwagon? Many people wait to contribute, either through volunteerism or monetarily, until the time is right—until they have enough money, time or energy. *The fact is that one will never have enough of these commodities until one determines how much is "enough."* Helping my clients figure out how much is enough is one of my more difficult, but rewarding, tasks as a financial services professional. To come up with a figure, the first thing a client needs to do is serious self-exploration to determine a satisfactory standard of living. For some, "satisfactory" means a couple of homes, high-end travel, private schools and all the up-to-date technical gadgets. For others, a comfortable home and a public college education for their children are adequate.

> Once a person figures out what they really need to be content, they can devote more of their time, energy, and money to charitable causes.

Regardless, once a person determines what they truly need to be content, they can devote more of their time, energy, and money to charitable causes. When freed from the constant concern of having enough money, people can accomplish miracles.

Creating a Disaster Relief Effort

In 1993, not long after my wife and I implemented the Zero Estate Tax Plan, severe flooding hit Des Moines, Iowa. On a whim, I gathered a few friends and we drove to the area to help an acquaintance whose place of business was destroyed. We helped clean up the soaked debris in the office and prepare it for the long re-building process. Motivated by the psychic income we received from providing hands-on assistance after a disaster, we gathered again shortly after to help clean up the wreckage in the yards of homes in a Minneapolis suburb following a tornado. The degree to which we could really help, however, was severely limited by the fact that we were equipped only with rakes!

On the ride home, we decided if we wanted to continue to assist in this way, we needed to bring good quality tools. We envisioned showing up at a disaster site with a trailer filled with tools we could use and loan to the local victims and volunteers in the affected area. Knowing my long-term financial obligations were satisfied, and that I was free to use my other assets as I wished, it was an easy decision for me to donate $25,000 of stock (received from a demutualization) to the cause (the stock had no tax basis). We used the money to build a tool trailer, equipped with power washers, wet/dry vacs, chainsaws, trash pumps, generators, and myriad other tools. It took a total of $25,000 to launch Nechama-Jewish Response to Disaster, the primary Jewish community response to natural disasters in the upper Midwest. (*"Nechama"* is Hebrew for "comfort").

Fast-forward to 2006: Nechama is now a 501(c)(3) non-profit organization with an annual budget of $150,000, and 2½ years of expenses in reserve. We employ a full-time director, employment manager and volunteer coordinator. We have several hundred volunteers in our database. We have three fully-equipped tool trailers and two other supply trailers. Nechama volunteers have made over 60 deployments to disaster areas in the Midwest since 1993 and spent 25 weeks in the Gulf Coast cleaning up after Hurricanes Katrina and Rita. I have an enormous sense of pride knowing that Nechama has made a difference in the lives of so many people, including those whose lives we help to repair as well as those who choose to volunteer their time with us. This is what can happen with a modest financial contribution, a vision, determination and the help of so many people willing to step forward and give of their resources.

We Need More Ingenuity and Compassion

If some of these stories haven't motivated you to reevaluate your charitable activities, let me try another angle. Before the government began assisting with the care of the disadvantaged and the elderly, that obligation fell on family members who, oftentimes, lacked the necessary funds or ability to take on this responsibility. This stifled societal/economic growth, as potential innovators and entrepreneurs spent many of their non-working hours caring for family members.

When some of this responsibility shifted to government agencies, our society prospered enormously as our great thinkers were free to do what they did best: develop industries that would lead to economic prosperity and create opportunities for millions of Americans.

> # We need the generosity revolution to take over where the capabilities of the government leave off.

As the national cost of providing care increased, the government raised taxes as a means of funding these necessary services. In response, Congress enacted laws to provide tax deductions to encourage charitable giving, a move that acknowledged *the inherent societal benefits of voluntary redistribution of wealth*. I think it would be detrimental for our nation to revert back to a system that required family members to take on sole responsibility for the care of their sick and elderly. This warning is of crucial importance now, as we face increased life expectancies, which will undoubtedly be accompanied by an increased need for nursing home or in-home care for the elderly. Societies assuming communal responsibility for their most vulnerable have a greater capacity for growth. We need the generosity revolution to take over where the capabilities of the government leave off. The government can provide the basic needs, but it takes the ingenuity of the American people to conceive of the endless possibilities to assist our most vulnerable citizens.

Claire Gaudiani speaks to this issue in her highly acclaimed book, *The Greater GOOD: How Philanthropy Drives the American Economy and Can Save Capitalism*. In it, she argues that capitalism and democracy coexist in America better than in any other country. The reason? Gaudiani credits the widely held American value of generosity for allowing democracy and generosity to not only coexist, but thrive in our society. In particular, Gaudiani is an advocate for the highest form of charity first suggested by 12th Century Jewish philosopher, Maimonides, in his Eight Stages of Tzedakah (loosely, and erroneously, translated from Hebrew as "charity", more accurately translated as "justice"). The highest level of giving, according to Maimonides, is to enter into a partnership with the recipient. Specifically, Gaudiani suggests that helping the poor to build wealth is the way to "jumpstart philanthropy and our economy" in the 21st Century. She proposes three broad categories in which to focus our wealth-building assistance to the poor:

1. Help increase home ownership for low-income families to generate equity development and wealth accumulation for current and future generations.

2. Invest in community centers in low-income areas. This supplements home ownership by increasing property values and wealth of low-income home owners.

3. Invest in children, who constitute 20% of our population, but 100% of our future.

What are YOU Doing for Charity?

In the next chapter, my friend and colleague Yale Levey will offer you valuable information on the "nuts and bolts" of becoming charitably involved. Meanwhile, I challenge each of you to arm yourself with your entrepreneurial spirit and ingenuity and join the Generosity Revolution. The opportunities are endless and the rewards are unparalleled.

Why not choose your area of interest and start up your own non-profit organization?

Why not choose your area of interest and start up your own non-profit organization? This idea is perfect for the entrepreneur. Starting Nechama-Jewish Response to Disaster has been one of the most rewarding experiences of my life. Not ready for such a big commitment? Consider chairing the strategy or implementation committee of an existing non-profit. Concerned about money? Remember to determine how much you need to create family security and contentment, and be generous with the rest!

Toss a stone in the generosity pool and see how far the ripples will go. You will be amazed. I leave you with these prolific words from Anne Frank: *"How wonderful it is that nobody needs to wait a single moment before starting to improve the world."*

◆◆◆

Steven Lear, ChFC, CLU, began his career in 1980 at American Express Financial Services. In 1989, he founded his own firm, Lear Financial Group, which then merged into Affiance Financial, LLC in 2000. Steve works with individuals and small businesses in the areas of financial planning, investment and insurance planning, estate planning, asset allocation, and retirement planning. Steve believes that his primary purpose as a financial consultant is to help people organize their finances and estates, so they can concentrate their time and energy on family, work, philanthropy, and leisure activities. Most recently, Steve has devoted his time and energy to encourage other financial services providers to adopt a philanthropic perspective, and in 2005 he founded The Philanthropic Will Company™, providing charitable gift tools for financial services providers.

Steve is a member of the *Financial Planning Association, Minnesota,* former board member of the *Twin Cities Chapter,* and a lifetime member of the *Million Dollar Round Table.* He was recognized by the Financial Network Investment Corporation as *Outstanding Representative of the Year (1999)* and received the *Circle of Achievement Award* (1996) in recognition for his community service. Steve also is the founder of *Nechama,* a volunteer disaster relief organization. He can be reached at: Affiance Financial LLC, 10275 Wayzata Blvd, Ste 300, Minnetonka, MN 55305; (tel) 952.253.2564; (email) stevelear@affiancefinancial.com.

Avoiding the Tax Sting
With Charitable Giving

Yale Levey, Managing Director
Roseland Financial Group, LLC*

Hopefully, after having just read the previous chapter, you are beginning to look at charity and philanthropy in a different way than before. Through his examples in Chapter 10, my friend, Steve Lear, has made a very strong case for why including philanthropy in our lives enhances us. Not only personally (our values, our virtues) but also socially (the causes and institutions we're passionate about). He has also shown us how incorporating philanthropy into our worlds actually serves as a catalyst to enhance our communities. Enhancements that include the creation of new businesses, new opportunities, and a greater amount of pride and accomplishment. Life enhancements that actually create wealth for us all.

In this chapter, I'd like to expand on those ideas by helping you understand how to best leverage your financial wealth to enhance your personal values and the social causes you're passionate about. The great news is, our tax code is set up in such a way that if we're proactive in our philanthropy (what I call voluntary philanthropy) as opposed to reactive in our philanthropy (what I call, involuntary philanthropy or, default to the IRS philanthropy) we actually can create more financial wealth for ourselves, often leave more financial wealth to our family, and, create much more personal and social wealth to support the causes and institutions we are passionate about.

Through tax avoidance and tax incentive opportunities, the IRS and thus, our tax code, actually has

*Securities products and investment advisor services offered through Royal Alliance Associates Inc., Member NASD/SIPC and a Registered Investment Advisor.

incentives built into it that can help you create more wealth than you might otherwise net yourself without including charity in your planning.

Through skilled planning techniques, it's possible for you to arrange your planning in such a way that, in the end, you and your family could actually yield more financially by including charity in your plans than if you hadn't.

You might be thinking, "That sounds almost too good to be true." Which is exactly what I thought when I first encountered this concept as a professional—finding that skilled planners have been helping people to plan this way for a long time. I'm not suggesting that, because of a deduction, a single current outright gift to charity will yield you more wealth than if you hadn't made the gift at all. I am saying that through skilled planning techniques, it's possible for you to arrange your financial affairs in such a way that, in the end, you and your family could actually yield more financially by including charity in your plans than if you hadn't. Pretty cool, huh!

When considering how this type of planning will work for you, it's important to know the financial ramifications of your gift. You need to identify the type of property you intend to give and the type of charitable organization you intend to give to. Has the asset increased above the original cost? All these things come into play. Entire books have been written on these topics alone. However, to simplify the basic financial benefits of charitable giving strategies, I won't be getting into all the nuances and complexities. Instead, let's assume that the upcoming examples I discuss with you are financially acceptable charitable gifts in the eyes of the IRS. Keep in mind, though, that before you implement any planning you should discuss all components of your intended planning with your advisors to ensure that you're compliant with the rules regarding deductibility of your gifts.

Some Of The Most Popular Tools People Use

I. Charitable Remainder Trusts

A charitable remainder trust (CRT) is a vehicle that allows you to leave a gift to charity after having used the trust asset as an income source for a particular period of time. For this reason, charitable remainder trusts are known as "split interest gifts". Split in that, you or someone you choose gets the income now, the charity gets the gift later.

Typically, CRTs are used by donors that wish to give property to charity but who don't wish to relinquish all use of the property right away. Often you may see a single donor, or a couple, perhaps a husband and wife, gift an asset into a CRT, then take an income stream from the asset for life or a term of years.

There are two main types of CRTs, a charitable remainder annuity trust (CRAT) and a charitable remainder unit trust (CRUT). Both have unique characteristics, but at their core, they share certain essential similarities.

Both provide for an income distribution to be paid to a non-charitable beneficiary. The income is to be paid no less than annually, for life or a specific term of years (not to exceed 20 years), with an irrevocable remainder interest that is held for the benefit of, or paid directly to, a charity. The remainder interest payable to charity must be no less than 10 percent of the original fair market value of the gift made into the trust (in the case of a CRAT) or 10 percent of the anticipated remainder value (in the case of a CRUT). Both types of CRTs have minimum and maximum income percentage requirements which are payable to the income beneficiary (five percent minimum, 50 percent maximum). In the case of a CRAT, it's a fixed percentage of the original gift made into the trust. In the case of a CRUT, the income payment is based on the value of the trust at the end of the year. Therefore, a CRUT must be re-valued at least annually to determine the amount of the income payments to the non-charitable beneficiary. Because of this difference, a CRUT can accept additional contributions, whereas a CRAT cannot. The CRAT can only accept a "sum certain," which is the original amount placed in trust. Additionally, there are different types of CRUTs, which are more sophisticated and provide even more flexibility by comparison to a CRAT. However, for simplicity sake, we won't discuss those here.

Both types of CRTs provide the donor with a current income tax deduction equal to the present value of the remainder interest that the charity will eventually receive. Essentially, a calculation is applied which takes into account several different factors (life expectancy of the donor, amount of income, rates of interest, etc.) Then, the assumed income payments are subtracted from the value of the gift to determine the remainder interest.

Like outright gifts to charity, gifts made to CRTs also avoid taxation on long-term capital gains. Therefore, it's not uncommon to see a donor gift a highly appreciated long-term gain asset into a CRT, sell it, and then take an income stream for life or a specific term of years. Not only do you avoid the capital gains tax, but you also get an income tax deduction.

It's because of these benefits that philanthropically-minded individuals who don't want to give up the income potential of an asset during retirement, but who ultimately want to give back to society, are particularly well-suited candidates for this kind of tool.

II. Charitable Lead Trusts

A charitable lead trust (CLT) provides that an income stream be paid to a qualifying tax-exempt organization for a donor's life, or a pre-specified time frame (which, unlike a CRT can be more than 20 years), typically at the end of which time, the remaining principle typically reverts back to the original grantor, or to a person of his or her choice. In terms of a CLT set up under the will of a grantor, the property would revert to the original grantor's chosen beneficiary.

There are two main kinds of charitable lead trusts. The first is known as a grantor CLT, the second a non-grantor CLT. Additionally, charitable lead trusts can be implemented during life (known as a lifetime CLT) or at death (known as a testamentary CLT). Let's talk about each.

A lifetime grantor charitable lead trust is named as such because the grantor does not intend on parting from the property gifted into trust indefinitely. Rather, the grantor places his property in trust, during which time, an income stream (whether it be an annuity income stream or a unitrust income stream) is payable to a qualifying charitable beneficiary organization. At the end of the predetermined time period (i.e. five years, 10 years, etc.), the property placed in trust reverts back to the grantor or remainderman of his choice. For income-tax purposes, the trust assets are viewed as if owned by the grantor and, as such, all trust income is taxable to the trust's grantor. This tool is often used when a grantor is interested in getting a large tax deduction in the year the trust is implemented. The grantor is entitled to take the present value of the future charitable gifts as a current income tax deduction. If, for example, the grantor happens to be expecting a rather large tax liability in any given year, funding assets in a grantor CLT can help to offset some of that tax liability. And, when the grantor is already charitably inclined, he or she can continue to support the causes and institutions that he or she would normally be inclined to support anyway.

The tax benefit the grantor receives is realized the year the trust is implemented.

It is important to note that the tax benefit the grantor receives is realized the year the trust is implemented. In a grantor CLT, there are no additional deductions for the income payments paid to charities during the term of the trust. Additionally, the grantor is responsible to pay the tax liability on whatever taxes the trust incurs during the term of the trust. Unlike a CRT, CLTs do not have a minimum five percent or maximum 50 percent payout stipulation. Of course, the percentage payout of the trust will affect the amount of deduction the grantor is able to take at the inception of the trust. Like CRTs, CLTs can be set up as annuity trusts or unitrusts, with similar rules. In a CLAT (annuity trust), the income payments are based on either a fixed-dollar amount or fixed percentage of the original amount funded into the trust, and no additional contributions can be made into the trust after it has been implemented. In a CLUT (unitrust), since the income payments are based on a fixed percentage of the trust value at the end of the year, additional payments can be made into the trust.

Where a lifetime grantor CLT provides an income tax deduction for the grantor, a testamentary CLT provides for an estate tax deduction for the grantor's estate when the grantor dies. So, in the case where a grantor is likely to have a significant estate tax liability, having a testamentary CLT in place can save a lot of estate taxes. (See the Jackie O. case study further in this chapter.) Of course the grantor's chosen beneficiary will have to wait until the end of the charitable term before they inherit the property placed in the testamentary CLT, but if the beneficiary has sufficient means to support themselves until the end of the term, this is a great tool.

The second type of CLT is known as a non-grantor CLT. A non-grantor CLT is one in which the grantor is not treated as owner of the trust for income tax purposes. Since a trust is not an individual, certain percentage limitations that apply to individuals do not apply here. Therefore, this type of trust is used when the donor/grantor wishes to make contributions in excess of percentage limitations that would normally affect individual taxpayers.

What makes this form of CLT very different from that of a grantor CLT is that the grantor does not get an income tax deduction at the time the trust is created and funded, and is not subject to the income taxes that the trust incurs annually. On the contrary, the income that the trust generates annually is fully deductible to the trust.

The gift tax due on the gift to family is based on the fair market value of the asset when first placed in trust, not at the end of the term.

These types of trusts are normally seen when a grantor wishes to transfer assets to someone other than themselves (i.e. their family) while minimizing the gift tax implications. This is because there is a gift tax deduction received for the present value of the annuity income stream the charity will be receiving.

Donors will sometimes use these types of trusts when they own an asset they intend on passing to family that they anticipate will be significantly appreciating in value in the future. The gift tax due on the gift to family is based on the fair market value of the asset when first placed in trust, not at the end of the term. Therefore, any appreciation the asset realizes while in the CLT will pass to heirs without any additional gift tax liability. (There may be generation-skipping taxes, though, in the case of an asset being inherited by a grandchild or great-grandchild.)

III. Charitable Gift Annuities

A charitable gift annuity is an investment that provides a donor with an income stream for life or a term of years, and at the end of that time period, the balance is paid to a charity. The gift into the annuity is treated like a bargain sale, or a sale in which the donor agrees to sell the asset to the charity at a discounted price.

In a gift annuity arrangement (CGA), the charity enters into a contract with the donor whereby, essentially, the charity agrees to pay the donor an income stream, typically, for the balance of the donor's life, at which time the charity's obligation to pay the annuity income ends. The charity bears all liability regarding paying the donor their predetermined income payments. Therefore, the donor need not worry about investment performance or outliving their money. They are assured to get an income they can't outlive, leave a legacy, and at the end of the day, support a cause that's dear to them.

Donors receive an income tax deduction when buying a CGA. The deduction is based on several factors but, essentially, the donor is able to get a deduction for the excess amount he or she is gifting to charity above the annuity income they are receiving. The age of the donor, IRS published interest rates, and actuarial calculations all serve to determine what the income payments and tax deduction will amount to.

Depending upon the type of asset the donor gives to the charity, they may also be able to receive very favorable tax treatment on the income stream received from the charity.

Depending upon the type of asset the donor gives to the charity, they may also be able to receive very favorable tax treatment on the income stream received from the charity. For example, if you gift an appreciated asset to a charity for purchase of a gift annuity, when the asset is sold, you don't realize capital gains tax liability on the sale in that tax year. Rather, when you receive your income, a portion of what you get annually will be taxed to you at capital gains tax rates, a portion will be taxed at regular ordinary income tax rates, and a portion will be considered your own principle and thus, no tax will be due on that portion.

IV. Private Foundations

Private foundations (aka private charities and/or 30 percent organizations) offer donors a way to keep far more control over their charitable capital than occurs when donating directly to a public charity. Therefore, they tend to be a favored choice for people who want to have a lot of control over the use of their gifts. When you give to a public charity, you relinquish control over your gift at the point you give it away.

Here are some of the typical reasons people start private foundations:

- The donor has a desire to create a more permanent legacy, perhaps something unique relating to their personal values.
- The donor wants to share their values and their vision with their children. (Private family foundation assets can remain in the foundation for generations.)
- The donor has a desire to maintain flexibility. (Foundation members control who get grants and have flexibility to change their minds.)
- The donor has a desire to maintain ongoing legal control over their charitable assets. (In a public charity, once you make the gift, you relinquish control over the gift.)
- The donor has a desire to give, yet remain anonymous. (Gifts to public charity are not always anonymous.)
- The donor has a steady or growing income above their personal needs. (A growing percentage of our country has acquired more than they need to live just for lifestyle.)
- The donor intends on endowing a foundation at death. (Think of Warren Buffet. He realized it was better to give it to a foundation now and enjoy the results of his gift now, while alive, rather than waiting until he died.)

There are four different types of private foundations:

1. *A non-operating foundation* – This is normally created by an individual or family and is not directly engaging in charitable activities, but makes grants to other charitable organizations. In this type of foundation, the donor can support philanthropic causes without actually having to run a charity. Not surprisingly, this is the most popular and widely used private foundation.

2. *A private operating foundation* – This type looks and acts very much like a public charity. They operate like a business and have various income tests, assets, endowments, and support tests.

3. *A pass-through foundation* – In this type, all contributions must pass through to another charitable organization shortly after having re-

ceived the contributions. Basically, the ultimate recipient organization handles the management of the charitable activities.

4. *A company-sponsored foundation.* This is one in which a for-profit corporation sets up a foundation, usually run by its directors or partners, and builds an endowment for future corporate contributions to support charitable organizations.

V. Wealth Replacement Trusts

One of the most important tools used in charitable estate and financial planning is the wealth replacement trust (WRT).

As discussed earlier, several of the tools involve the irrevocable gift of an asset either directly to charity, to a charitable trust, for purchase of a charitable gift annuity, or, to a charitable private foundation. In all of these instances, a gift is being made to charity and thus, not being given to the family or other beneficiaries of the donor outright. Although several of these tools enable the donor, and/or the donor's beneficiary to get a significantly increased income stream, ultimately, what's left over for family at the end of the day will go to charity.

Another important point is that in many instances, donors who are implementing tools such as those described have estates that are large enough to subject the donor and their family to sizable estate taxes once the donor passes away.

The wealth replacement trust and subsequent life insurance purchased within the wealth replacement trust address both of these issues.

A standard wealth replacement trust is an irrevocable trust, which normally is funded with assets (usually cash or securities) most commonly used to purchase life insurance on one or more persons' lives. The trust is the owner of the life insurance and the trust is the beneficiary of the life insurance. The insured, typically the parent or parents, do not own or control the insurance, nor do the kids. The person acting as trustee for the trust is responsible for the purchase and maintenance of the life insurance. Upon the death of the insured, the life insurance proceeds are payable to the trust; and, since life insurance proceeds are income tax free, no taxes are due upon the payment into the trust.

So what is the intended result in using a tool like this? Well, when the donor made the gift into the CRT, or charitable gift annuity, or private foundation, they irrevocably parted with the ownership of that asset. They may own the income stream for the rest of their lives payable from those other planning tools, but they irrevocably parted with the principle. The wealth replacement trust serves to replace that principle, either in part or in whole, to the donor's family or beneficiary of their choice. At the end of the day, they've accomplished their charitable intentions while still leaving their family "financially" whole.

The Periodic Table of Estate Planning Elements

We use this table to help in discussions with you and the planning team members as to which tools should be considered from among the wide universe of available strategies and programs.

Charitable Remainder Uni-Trust	Charitable Remainder Annuity Trust	LLC/CRTs	Private Annuity	Grantor Retained Annuity Trust	ILIT	Leveraged Bonus Plan
TCLAT	Gift Annuity	Family Limited Partnerships	Principal Protected Notes	Sale for Installment Note	Restricted Management Account	Offshore Captive Planning
Charitable Life Estate	NIMCRUT	Long Term Care Insurance	529 Plans	Gifting	Asset Protection	QPRTs
Private Foundations	FLIPCRUT	Walton GRAT	Family LLC	Annuity Withdrawal	SPIA/Life Arbitrage	ESOP Planning
SPIA/Life in a CLAT	CLUT	Revocable Living Trusts, DPAs	Crummey Powers	Dynasty Trust	Corporate Recapitalization	412(I)
Supporting Organizations	CLAT	Preferred LPs	Jurisdictional Trusts	Premium Finance	SCIN	IRA Maximizer
Bargain Sales	Donor Advised Funds	Life Insurance	Succession Planning	Buy-Sell Planning	GDOT	Qualified Plan Limited Partnership

■ Charitable Planning Tools   ▨ Personal Planning Tools   ▨ Qualified Planning Tools

Case Histories, Real and Hypothetical

Case Study #1 – Sale of a highly appreciated public stock to create the following scenarios:

- Increased income stream you can't outlive

- Sizable upfront tax deductions

- Avoidance of all capital, estate and gift taxes

- Bequest a sizable legacy to charity

- Opportunity to pass on your values

- Support causes you care about

- Conversion of assets to a tax-free inheritance for surviving family

The Dilemma: Vicki and Stephen are a married couple. They have accumulated a net worth of $15 million dollars. Some of their assets are in real estate, some are tied up in a family business, some are in municipal bonds and they have (are you ready?) a highly appreciated stock that Stephen originally bought for $25,000 and now it's worth $1,500,000 (he was smart enough to put $25,000 in Home Depot the year it came out!). They are aware that although they have done very well with this stock, having that much in one asset is not a good idea. It's a poor financial planning strategy. However, if they sell the stock, they will have to pay capital gains taxes on the gain (roughly $225,000). So, it's like locked-up capital. They don't want to sell it, but they don't want to keep that much in one investment, either.

Stephen, more than anyone I know, hates paying taxes. He's also concerned that if he predeceases Vicki that she will have enough income to live on. They would both like to leave as much as possible to family and convert their taxes to charitable giving if possible. They are both 78 years old; they have three kids and seven grandkids and are in good health. Additionally, they both still work in the family business that Stephen's father started. Their adjusted gross income (AGI) taken from the business is $400,000 per year and their combined federal and state income tax bracket rate is 45 percent.

The Solution: Rather than selling the stock outright and paying the capital gains tax on $1.475 million of gain ($225,000), they decide to gift the stock into a CRUT and then sell it. Now they get to reinvest the entire $1.5 million. The proceeds will be reinvested into a diverse portfolio of investments (this will take care of their asset allocation problem). The trust will pay them eight percent, before tax, on the value of the trust at the end of the year for the rest of their lives. Their stock is currently paying a dividend of about 1.75 percent before tax, or $26,250 per year taxable dividend on the $1.5 million. At eight percent, their initial income will be $120,000 pre-tax per year, an increase of about $94,000 per year.

Additionally, at their ages, 78, they will qualify for a current income tax deduction of about $590,000 which can be used to shield taxes. In their tax bracket, this will save them about $265,000 of income taxes (current law may require them to realize this savings over as much as a five-year time period, depending upon their income). The CRT they create states that upon the death of the second spouse, half the money will be paid outright to the Jewish Community Center, an organization Vicki cares about deeply, the other half will go into a family-controlled foundation. This will allow their kids to continue supporting the causes and institutions Vicki and Stephen care about, as well as other qualifying charities the kids choose to support.

Now, as if this wasn't good enough, here's where it gets really interesting.

They have their attorney draft a wealth replacement trust in which they gift about $40,000 per year (this figure assumes they qualify for preferred non-smoker rates) that they take from the $120,000 income they receive from the CRT, enough to fund the premium payment on a $1.5 million life insurance policy on both of their lives and payable at the second death. They are still netting about $80,000 in pre-tax income even after the cash gift into the wealth replacement trust. That's more than three times the income they were getting from the Home Depot stock. The trust provisions allow for the $1.5 million to be paid outright to their kids upon the second death.

Finally, it's important to note the estate tax savings: With a $15 million dollar estate, the federal estate tax liability on the $1.5 million of Home Depot stock would have been about $700,000 or almost half given current estate tax liability. Additionally, since life insurance, if owned appropriately, pays its proceeds income tax free, there are no income taxes due from the kids when the wealth replacement trust pays out the life insurance proceeds to them.

Summary of Benefits

- Save approximately $490,000 of income and capital gains taxes during their lives ($225,000 from capital gains and $265,000 from income taxes)

- Increase first year pre-tax income by about $54,000 per year ($120,000 —$40,000 cost of insurance versus stock dividend of $26,250)

- Approximately $700,000 in estate tax savings given current tax laws

- Dramatic increase in lifetime income (about $54,000 pre-tax income in the first year and an income stream thereafter)

- Heirs receive the full $1,500,000 tax free

- Together, with ongoing family involvement, become philanthropists of the original $1,500,000 gift into the trust.

- Ultimately, and maybe most importantly, gain comfort, clarity and confidence to move forward, and support the causes that they value while enhancing their retirement income.

Did they have more when they finished than when they started? Yes!

Case Study #2 – **Use of a charitable gift annuity as a supplement to retirement income, and a way to support a cause that you're passionate about.**

Dilemma: Evelyn is an 80-year-old widow. She has no children and intends to leave a substantial portion of her estate to charity after she passes away. Although she has a nest egg to provide for herself in the event she has any unforeseen emergencies, she still worries that not enough income will be generated from her assets to support her lifestyle. She likes the comfort that fixed income investments like CD's and bonds provide her; but, she's very unsatisfied with the current rate of interest she gets for her money. Evelyn likes to spend her spare time helping out at a charity called Eva's Village, that feeds, houses and offers medical care for homeless people. She intends to recognize Eva's through a bequest in her will.

Solution: Evelyn should consider investing a portion of her assets into a charitable gift annuity (CGA) sponsored by Eva's Village in lieu of, or in addition to, the money she intends on leaving them in her will. If she enters into a gift annuity contract with Eva's, at her age she will likely receive an income stream of approximately 10 percent per year for the rest of her life. Eva's will be contractually obligated to pay Evelyn this income until she passes away. After she dies, whatever is left will remain with Eva's. The interest she will receive is almost double what she can expect to get on a safe bond or CD given what interest rates on investments of this type are paying today.

Case Study #3[1] – **Help the kids earn it by using charitable lead trusts!**

The Dilemma: Sally wants her children to earn their way in life so they will have a sense of pride and positive self-esteem, which she has been teaching them since birth. She does not want them to be "trust babies." She also wants them to set a good example for her yet-to-be-born grandkids, so the future grandkids will model their lives after high self-esteem parents and will be productive members of society. Sally also believes control of assets, not necessarily ownership, equates to power in the business world.

Sally and her deceased husband had done preliminary estate planning. They set up a wealth replacement trust, which purchased a $2.5 million of second-to-die life insurance on their lives. Those insurance proceeds will be estate tax exempt. Sally has a $10 million estate.

The Solution: At her death, Sally's living trust (where her assets are held now) will transfer the $10 million into a testamentary CLT that will pay out eight percent for 10 years to charity, entitling her to a $5,480,664 estate tax charitable deduction. Her taxable estate will be $4,519,336 ($10 million - $5,480,664) and her estate taxes will be $2,259,668. The $800,000 per year distribution will be paid to a private foundation and become the principal (the endowment) of the foundation. Over 10 years, $8 million will accumulate in the private foundation. At an eight percent projected rate of return, the foundation will have $640,000 (8% x $8 million) to give to public charities each year.

Sally doesn't want her children to have access to the estate for 10 years—she wants them to become "lean and mean." After the 10-year charitable term, the income from the $10 million will be held in trust and paid out as part of a "matching grant" program: that is, each year the trust will pay to each of Sally's children an amount of income that matches the amount of personal income earned that year by the child (or the child's spouse should the child stays home to raise the children). If a child (or spouse) does not earn anything, then the child receives no income from Sally's trust that year. At the age of 65, Sally's kids can retire and collect all trust income.

Here is the engine that drives this estate plan. Sally's children will be the trustees of the private foundation and control the distribution of the $640,000 yearly payments to public charities. If Sally's children carefully select the appropriate charities, the children will be appointed to the boards of directors of significant public charities in the areas in which they live. Doing so will allow them to network at the highest level of society. This networking will allow the children to advance their business careers, and matching grants from Sally's $10 million trust will augment the money made from their business careers. The foundation is the children's "admission ticket to prominence and stature in society," and for Sally's grandchildren, great-grandchildren, and so on. That is because the private foundation never terminates.

---

[1]Excerpts of this case were taken from material provided by the American College for its CAP program. Original article was written by Steven L. Gleitman and was reprinted with permission by the Financial Planning Association, *Journal of Financial Planning*. December, 1995, Steven L Gleitman, "A Practice Guide to Charitable Lead Trusts."

The insurance trust (wealth replacement trust) will receive $2.5 million in insurance proceeds, sufficient to pay the roughly $2.25 million estate taxes. Sally's children will control $18,240,332 with the CLT compared with $7.5 million ($10 million - $5 million in estate taxes + the $2.5 million insurance proceeds) without the CLT. If Sally and her deceased husband had not set up the insurance trust, her estate would not be able to pay the estate taxes. In that case, this strategy would not work unless she established an insurance trust that would purchase a $2.5 million policy on her life that would be exempt from estate tax.

Here are my summarized conclusions of benefits Sally's heirs will receive as taken from the original case study:

- *Sally's estate taxes*

    Gross Estate = $10,000,000

    Charitable Deduction = ($5, 480,664)

    Taxable Estate = $4,519,336

    Estate Tax at 50% = $2,259,668

- *Assets To Children*

    Gross Estate = $10,000,000

    Insurance to children = $2,500,000

    Estate Taxes = ($2,259,668)

    Total assets in trust for children if Sally were to die now = $10,240,332 versus $7,500,000 the kids would have gotten outright.

- *Assets in private foundation*

    $8,000,000 ($800,000/year for 10 years)

- *Assets controlled by children at end of the term*

    $18,240,332

Case Study #4[2] – Jackie O's Charitable Lead Annuity Trust: The C&J Foundation

Jackie O's will put her residuary estate in a trust—The C&J Foundation (Carolyn and John). Mrs. Onassis's will calls the arrangement a foundation, but it is a charitable lead annuity trust and it still smells sweet for the charities that will benefit handsomely for 24 years. And the estate tax and generation-skipping tax savings are fragrant too.

Here are the provisions of the plan I've summarized from the original case study:

- Payment to charity: An eight percent annuity income stream gets paid to charity for 24 years.

[2]Excerpts of this case were taken from material provided by the American College for its' CAP program. Original article was written by Conrad Teitell and was reprinted from *Trusts and Estates*, September 1994, Intertec Publishing Corp. Reproduced with permission of the publisher via the Copyright Clearance Center, Inc..

- Selecting the charities: Payments are to be made to qualified "public" charities (not a private foundation) selected by her trustees, but she does mention her preference favoring cultural organizations and charities that support the betterment of mankind and the relief of suffering.

- Remainder to family members: At the end of the 24-year term, the assets are to be distributed to family members.

- The trustees: Mrs. Onassis's daughter, Caroline B. Kennedy, her son John F. Kennedy, Jr., Alexander D. Forger and Maurice Tempelsman are the trustees.

- JOLT's estate tax charitable deduction. We do not know the value of Mrs. Onassis's residuary estate that will fund the charitable lead annuity trust. Based on press reports, let us assume a $100 Million residuary estate (a nice round number). Jackie O. died in May 1994. If we assume the most favorable deduction calculation was applied to her assets, the estate tax charitable deduction for a $100 million charitable lead trust paying charities $8 Million a year for 24 years is approximately $96.8 Million. So only $3.2 million of the $100 million trust will be subject to estate tax in Jackie O's estate. Again, the value of the residuary estate is assumed. Whatever the value, however, the estate tax charitable deduction will equal approximately 96.80% of the amount funding the charitable lead trust.

Looking down the road, the generation-skipping tax will be payable at the end of the 24-year term. The amount depends on the value of the trust at the time and the then-effective interest assumptions. Assuming 1) the trust was funded with $100 million; 2) it uses the lowest allowable monthly discount rate – 6.40 percent, the rate for March, 1994; 3) it earns eight percent per year and appreciates two percent annually; and, 4) it makes annual end-of-the-year payments to charity, the value of the assets after 24 years will be approximately $213 million. The generation-skipping tax at that time would be (assuming that the GST is still in existence) approximately $115 million leaving the family with roughly $98.60 million dollars.

Conclusion

Incorporating charitable planning into one's overall financial plan is a goal that I, and many of my colleagues, would like to see become mainstream. As a matter of fact, I'd argue that these strategies are radically sane, yet not used often enough. My intention, and my hope, is that after having read this chapter, you'll begin to realize that this type of planning is possible for you. It's doable. It's accessible. You don't have to be a Mellon, a Rockefeller, a Carnegie, a Gates, or, a Buffet to make a major impact on the causes and institutions that you're passionate about. And, there are advisors out there who can help you to enhance not only your families' financial wealth, but also, in the planning, can help you enhance your personal wealth and your social wealth.

My job in this chapter was to pull from all of the many tools, techniques, options, opportunities and strategies, a few of the most commonly used ones, and then, to translate, into English, what these tools can do for you. In the end, hopefully to open your eyes and motivate you. I hope I was successful.

◆◆◆

Yale Levey is the founder and Managing Director of Roseland Financial Group, LLC. He is a nationally recognized financial educator, speaker and lecturer whom you may have seen interviewed by Robin Dorean on TV's "Wall Street Journal Weekend" or read about in the book *The Trust Equation, The Savvy Investor's Guide to Selecting a Competent, Ethical Financial Advisor.* He has also been interviewed by various industry publications including *Financial Planning Magazine* and *Wealth Manager Magazine*.

Yale has conducted hundreds of presentations across the country on topics including Reducing Income Taxes and Eliminating Estate Taxes, How to leave a Three Dimensional Legacy, Family Wealth Preservation, Tax Smart Retirement Planning and Ensuring your Families Future. In addition to investors, CPA's, attorneys and financial professionals at numerous firms have benefited from his instruction.

He is also both a Charter Member, and Board Member of the International Association of Advisors in Philanthropy (www.advisorsinphilanthropy.org), a national organization of like minded professionals dedicated to helping clients effectively direct their resources for the betterment of humankind consistent with their values.

Yale has counseled wealthy individuals throughout the country for almost two decades now. His advice and assistance have saved them Millions of dollars in estate, capital gains and income taxes. A Certified Financial Planner™ and a Chartered Advisor in Philanthropy™, Yale and his family make their home in South Orange, NJ.

Yale is a gifted communicator and has a passion for helping people think about their wealth from a new perspective—showing them how they can leave a legacy of not just their money, but also of their personal values and significant influence in their community.

Yale can be reached at Roseland Financial Group, LLC, 101 Eisenhower Parkway, Roseland, NJ 07068; (tel) 973.228.6566; (email) yale@roselandfinancialgroup.com; (website) www.roselandfinancialgroup.com.

Succession Planning
For Family Business Owners:
Improving the Odds for Success

Hugh B. Roberts, CFP®, Partner
The Rawls Group

Tired of the day-to-day grind of running your business? Thinking of retiring? The relevant question is how are you going to pull this off and still perpetuate a business that reflects a lifetime of hard work, creativity and sacrifice?

These are common, often troubling, questions asked by business owners. For some, retirement means, "I'm turning over the keys and going fishing, golfing, etc." However, for most business owners, retirement means, "I come and go when I want, leave the daily headaches to someone else and have more freedom to enjoy the fruits of my lifetime of work – but, I still want to be involved in the big decisions." This is often called "entrepreneurial retirement." The key to making either type of retirement work is having a succession plan in place.

"Succession planning? Yes, I've done that—I've got a will, buy-sell agreement and life insurance." This is the most common response from business owners who are asked about their succession planning. But if that's all you've done, your odds are terrible that you will be able to retire with peace of mind that your legacy will not become unraveled. Also, when you properly address succession planning, you can have the confidence that if you encounter a catastrophe before retirement the business will continue as an asset for your family and community. So, what is succession planning?

First, let's review that Succession Success[sm] as defined by my colleagues at The Rawls Group is the effective and efficient transfer of a business entity *through* the next generation of family members or partners. While wills, buy-sell agreements and life insurance are important elements of succession planning, these planning steps merely involve the transfer of the business *to* the next generation, but they have little to do with whether or not the business will survive and prosper 20 or 30 years after the transfer. Knowing this, succession planning is the process of addressing *all* the issues that will impact the succession and success of the business.

Only approximately 25% of all family businesses have a family member who is ready, willing and able immediately to succeed the business owner in the event of the owner's death.

It's your business—you are the master of your universe—but what are the odds that your business has a future after you are gone? *The facts are that most family-owned businesses will NOT succeed from one generation to another. Approximately 75% of family-owned businesses will NOT succeed through the second generation and over 90% from second to third generation.* It is also true that only approximately 25% of all family businesses have a family member who is ready, willing and able immediately to succeed the business owner in the event of the owner's death. Looking at these odds you must conclude that if your dream is to retire or just stop the daily grind and do what you want to do and see your legacy continue, then you will need to commit significant time, energy and resources to succession planning and the achievement of succession success.

Since the business is usually a business owner's most valuable asset, both financially and emotionally, why would business owners not commit to planning that would assure that his or her legacy continue after retirement and through the next generation? Obviously there are myriad reasons, depending on the individual, but often the reason is FEAR. And being the successful, strong, driving personality, you appropriately ask, fear of what?

- *Fear of Losing Control* – Most business owners are entrepreneurs because they like to be in control. Therefore, the thought of confronting any subject that involves giving up control to anyone, including their children, causes many business owners to back away from any planning.

  Addressing this fear involves achieving an understanding that there are three types of control: "legal control" (owning 51% of the stock), "golden hammer control" (he who has the gold has the hammer), and "Mom and Dad control" (out of love and respect you will do what I say). "Legal control" is the one most business owners cling to and, yet, most do not understand that if you have to use it, there could be a family disaster, even a court battle! That's not a pretty place for a family business owner. Often there can be less dependency upon legal control when a business owner recognizes that he can rule through his relationships. With "Dad control" he can impact decisions via his family's need for his financial resources (golden hammer control). Having said that, there are definitely situations identified in the succession planning process wherein a business owner's fear of giving up legal control is justified and should be protected. Carefully considering the need to retain legal control is an important subject for discussion with your advisors.

- ***Fear of Conflict with Your Spouse and/or Children*** – Many business owners know that their spouse and/or children feel differently about succession and assume succession planning will generate conflict. Dad may be looking at this issue as the business owner, while mom is approaching the issue as a mother. Consequently, there is often concern that the spouse will create more conflict by supporting children with unreasonable expectations about the commitment or competency required to assume leadership and command and allow you to retire with peace of mind. Predictably, this is a concern with a blended family. Your children, who often use conflict as a way of achieving their goals, may, without the support of mom, have an entirely different view of what they want to see happen. For instance, the children may want to assume control sooner than you are willing to step aside. Therefore, a common response to succession planning is, "Why stir up trouble if I don't have to?"

This legitimate fear requires outside help! Avoiding conflict often magnifies problems. But, no doubt, trying to navigate family emotions without an objective and experienced facilitator can be a recipe for disaster. It is often difficult to communicate with family members, especially on business-related emotionally charged issues. However, with the help of a facilitator who is adept at navigating the choppy waters of family communication, this fear can be reconciled and solutions can be found that work for your unique family.

- ***Fear of Regretting a Decision*** – Business owners know that so many things can happen—changes in the nature or profitability of your business, family changes, tax law changes, all of which lead to the fear that you might have made the wrong decision. Since this involves your life and life's work, plus in many cases, the family's security, it is easy to say, "I can't make these decisions now – I don't have enough information and I may make a mistake. I'll have to wait a few more years."

The fact is that succession plans should remain flexible and should be reviewed regularly in order to accommodate inevitable change. The longer you wait the more difficult the issues will be and the more expensive it will be to implement your plans. Therefore, start now and update regularly.

- ***Fear of the Unknown*** – This fear is similar to regretting a decision, but it also has to do with the business owner knowing intuitively that in order to retire and achieve his succession goals; there are a lot of complex issues which need to be addressed. The fear is that he doesn't know his options or the consequences of each decision.

It is crucial that you engage a team of experienced professionals who will develop an understanding of where you want to go, help you understand the implications of what you are going to encounter and who can help you consider the alternative avenues for retiring and achieving succession. By working as a team, your advisors should be able to clarify the diverse issues, alleviate your fears and help you achieve your planning objectives.

Based on these fears, it is easy to understand why succession planning is often put on the backburner, even though business owners readily admit that protecting their legacy is vitally important. When you have these doubts and fears in your mind, it is easy to see how you can allow the tyranny of the urgent issues of the business to cause them to procrastinate on this all-important issue.

With regard to succession planning, most business owners have experienced some type of fear, often inhibiting them from taking action. However, when these concerns are discussed with trained succession professionals, generally options and solutions are found that will allow you to move past these fears and accomplish your goals. So, once you are ready to move forward, how do you determine where you currently stand regarding the succession of your business?

How can you rate your business succession qualifications? The questionnaire on page 131, also available on the RawlsGroup.com website, is designed to give you a reading of the challenge you will be encountering in achieving succession success, i.e. the ability for the business to be successful through the next generation.

When you are finished, add your points to rate your business succession preparation:

90-105 points = Congratulations on your diligence.
80-89 points = Your planning may need review.
60-79 points = Your planning needs review. There is work that should be done.
40-59 points = There is definitely need for you to initiate planning.
20-39 points = Your goals are at great risk. Begin your planning right away.

Simple Questions that Can Lead to Important Conclusions
Circle a number to rate yourself on each question
(5=confidently addressed, 4=partially, 3=unsure, 2=don't know, 1=not addressed)

1. How prepared are you to be financial independent from the business? 1 2 3 4 5

2. Do you have a business succession implementation plan? 1 2 3 4 5

3. Have you communicated your succession goals/plan to family, bankers and franchisers and solicited their reaction and input? 1 2 3 4 5

4. Do you have a current "succession memo" describing what your family and key managers should do in the event of your sudden death or incapacitation? 1 2 3 4 5

5. Do you have a working family business council to facilitate intra-family communication and initiate group problem solving? 1 2 3 4 5

6. Do you have documented arrangements to continue compensation and benefits for you upon your retirement and your spouse in the event of your death? 1 2 3 4 5

7. How prepared are your children to be the successor owners/managers of the business? 1 2 3 4 5

8. How confident are you that your managers will continue to support your successor(s)? 1 2 3 4 5

9. How well have you restricted transfers of business interests in the event of divorce, bankruptcy, employment termination or irreconcilable differences between partners? 1 2 3 4 5

10. How confident are you that your trustees and executors can effectively manage the business and estate assets? 1 2 3 4 5

11. How well do you understand the impact estate taxes can have on equitable asset distribution, business operations and business succession? 1 2 3 4 5

12. How well do your children understand your estate continuity and business succession plans? 1 2 3 4 5

13. Have any significant events occurred that have not been appropriately addressed which could impact your succession planning, such as (subtract 1 point for each):
   o Change in health o Divorce o Marriage o Loss of a key person o Financial changes

14. How pleased are you with the terms of your wills and trusts? 1 2 3 4 5

15. How aware are you of the cost, publicity and administrative implications of probate? 1 2 3 4 5

16. Do you fully understand how trusts operate? 1 2 3 4 5

17. How comfortable are you with your plan for equitable distribution of your business and other assets? 1 2 3 4 5

18. How confident are you that your estate is structured for minimum estate tax cost? 1 2 3 4 5

19. Have you utilized unified gift tax credits for strategic business gifting? 1 2 3 4 5

20. Are you following a regular gifting program with regard to other assets? 1 2 3 4 5

21. How pleased are you with your life insurance portfolio and the manner in which your life insurance is being utilized? 1 2 3 4 5

The 10 Critical Succession Issues

My colleagues and I at The Rawls Group in collaboration with a panel of independent experts have identified 10 interdependent planning issues that are critical to the achievement of succession success. In order for you to retire and have peace of mind that your business can continue to succeed through the next generation, these issues should be addressed.

1. Personal Financial Planning

This fundamental succession planning consideration involves progressively utilizing the fruit of business success to achieve personal financial independence from your business. Financial independence provides you, the owner, freedom to sell the business for what it is actually worth versus the awkward, costly environment where attempts are made to sell the business to sustain personal security. Additionally, financial independence enables you to empower succession by incurring the inherent risk of relinquishing control of your business to family members or key managers.

With this definition in mind, let's get practical. You aren't about to relinquish major decision-making, much less control to others if all your financial eggs are in one basket. Since most business owners have grown their business by re-investing in the business, the net result is that you now own the real estate, inventory, have developed cash reserves in your business, all of which have created the growth of your business. This is a time-honored business growth formula, but it is a significant succession liability. Ideally, for succession the business owner would have sufficient net worth outside the business, thereby giving him the financial freedom to allow his children and managers to mature in the business, with the confidence that their potential mistakes will not threaten his lifestyle or financial security.

With regard to retirement, determining how much income you need and how dependent you are going to be on the profitability of the business, is essential. Therefore, a key recommendation will be to develop sufficient income independent from the business. The closer you get to achieving this goal, the greater the protection for your retirement and the succession of the business.

2. Business Structuring

Business structuring can also positively or negatively impact the succession of the business. In the event of a sale, the appropriate corporate or partnership structure would enable stockholders to build tax bases and avoid discouraging taxation on the sales proceeds. Appropriately designed and coordinated stockholder/partner agreements give participating principals the peace of mind that their interests in the business represents real value and that this value cannot be distorted by undesirable stockholder/

partners. Employment contracts can enhance exit strategies by authorizing the continuity of compensation and health benefits after retirement or to a spouse after death. The utility or liability of the business to you, the surviving family and key personnel will depend upon the appropriate business structures.

Space will not permit us to explore the numerous issues that need to be addressed, but let's look at a few. Shareholder agreements are an essential tool to ensure that only those you want to own stock will. These documents need to address what you want to happen in the event of death, disability, divorce, termination of employment or retirement. The key is to make these decisions when there is no adverse pressure and everyone can make prudent decisions. Failure to do so can create significant business and personal family problems and can be a factor in succession failure.

How you structure the ownership of the business real estate can have a profound effect on your succession plan. Ideally the business owner sets up the ownership of the real estate in an entity such as a limited liability company (LLC), which is separate from the business. This will provide you with a number of different succession planning options. Among these is the possibility of the business owner eventually transferring the business stock to his children who are active in the business, while keeping the real estate for his retirement and eventually, for his non-active children. An LLC also provides the option of gifting equity to your children while retaining control of the property. This can be very helpful in reducing estate taxes.

3. Business Performance

Operational success is the value magnet that will draw suitors and compel them to bid up the value of the asset. Operational success is also critical to achieving the profitability momentum required to endure predictable challenges to business continuity within your family. Operational success can, and usually does, come from a variety of sources such as great location, terrific product line or you just being a great operator.

The bottom line is that business is about making money. The process of transitioning leadership and management can challenge historical profitability. Unless your business has achieved an enduring, high level of profitability, it is predictable that succession will be a formidable challenge.

4. Strategic Planning

Succession planning is fundamentally a long-term strategic issue, and is critically important to your business succeeding through the next generation. Everyone understands the cliché, "If you fail to plan, you plan to fail." It is a given that your business will encounter serious challenges. Change will be your major obstacle and, notably, the transition of management control and leadership is a significant change. How you deal with change is a function of your forethought and preparation. All too often family businesses are so focused on the immediate challenges of running the business, that little or no attention is given to long-range planning, which is essential for succession.

5. Leadership and Management Continuity

Much of the value of a business is in the management team that optimizes resources for the achievement of business goals. Therefore, recruiting, training and empowering a management culture that can sustain and enhance historical success is imperative for a successful transition. The identification, motivation and retention of highly-qualified supporting managers are essential to maintaining the viability of succession plans. It is also important to look at those who can take it to the next level and begin developing them as key managers. Developing bench strength is important to the strength and sustainability of any team.

Business is all about good people functioning together for the betterment of the business. At the same time, business owners need to be aware of the goals and motivating factors for each of their key managers, particularly as it relates to succession planning. Will your managers be willing to stay when your son or daughter takes over? While you may think your people are so loyal that they would never leave, they will become very vulnerable to outside offers when you are no longer in the picture. Making sure these key managers have an economic reason ("golden handcuffs") to stay under the potential stress of succession transition, will be vital to your children continuing the success of the business.

6. Successor Preparation

Skill assessment, training, accountability and mentoring of family members is critical to building the proper management culture. Family members must be held to the same standards as any other applicant applying for a management position. Creating and communicating an expectation for entry into the business and/or management will ensure your successor will have proper training, will gain the respect of their colleagues, and communicate policy consistency.

"Help, I've got kids in the business!" is stated by all too many business owners. Self-made entrepreneurs often find it extremely frustrating as their hopes and dreams for their children succeeding them often fall far short of expectations. All too often, parents know what to do, but are unwilling to hold their children accountable to the same standards of non-family members. Unfortunately, the fear of damaging relationships with our children can often lead to significant destructive decisions, especially when family comes under the pressure of the family business environment.

7. Management Synergy and Teamwork

Organizational structure, lines of communication and levels of accountability are extremely important for success in a business environ-

---

Golden Rules Regarding Children Working in Your Business

For every one of these rules, there are plenty of exceptions in which a child has thrived, but these concepts are highly recommended:

• Develop a written family business employment policy — This will clearly state your requirements for family members to be hired into your business. Among these might include a college degree and successful full-time work experience for one year at another business.

• Adopt written family member employee expectations — Your children need to know specifically what is expected of them and that they will be under intense scrutiny when working in your business. The assumption is that they have the job only because they have the right genes and they will not be held to the same standards as others. They will have to refute this erroneous expectation and earn respect by working harder than others and maintaining a non-entitlement attitude. Don't assume they are aware of your expectations — write them down.

• Develop a three- to five-year training curriculum so they know how you expect to train them, and what is expected, including goals and measures of accountability.

• Utilize key managers to mentor your children and let these managers know precisely how you will respond when they need to hold your children accountable.

• Pay children based on the job they are performing, not based on equality with their siblings or what lifestyle you want them to enjoy. If you want them to receive more, provide this income from other sources such as dividends or real estate revenue.

• Do not promote too quickly — Allowing your child to take the elevator, not the stairs to the top can be disastrous. It is really hard to demote after promoting.

---

ment. The success of a business is dependent upon the quality and effectiveness of management. The quality of management is usually dependent upon the identification and positioning of talented and committed managers. The effectiveness of management is dependent upon how managers form a cohesive team and work collaboratively to achieve a unified mission. Synergy of management is a challenging but worthwhile goal that is a common component of those businesses that have prepared themselves and will succeed through the next generation.

Far too often "turf management" is the norm in family businesses, in which managers are guarding their "turf" and cooperating with other departments on a "what's in it for me" basis. Time and attention needs to be given to management, leadership and communication facilitation. Are your management meetings designed merely to communicate your thoughts or are they interactive and involve group problem solving and support?

Unfortunately, teamwork is not a natural behavior pattern. Your family and managers need training to learn how to subordinate personal short-term needs for the achievement of long-term group goals that ultimately generate benefits that far exceed expectations. Also, customized non-qualified deferred compensation plans can create incentives for teamwork and cooperation. Management teams that are incentivized to work together, improve profitability and make a career commitment are profound assets in the pursuit of succession success.

8. Family Dynamics

Effective interaction of family members is required to achieve the unity and harmony regarding the complex issues involved in a family business. Otherwise, bickering will undermine the intrinsic strength of the family business team. Effective intra-family communication is essential for the training and accountability that are required to develop successor/owner managers. Effective communication provides the building blocks for building a unified succession vision and taking the steps for the achievement of family business succession goals.

Unfortunately, many business owners would agree with the statement, "I do a great job of communicating with your children, but a so-so job of communicating with my own." No doubt, it is much more difficult to relate to our children due to the emotional baggage, expectations, history, concern over the consequences, etc. As one business owner said while considering promoting his son to the general manager of the business, "I'm excited and scared to death!" "How will I hold him accountable and what if I have to fire him?" Let's face it—the stakes are much higher when dealing with your children!

Since communication with family members is often delicate, it is recommended that clearly written expectations be developed between the business owner and active children in the business. These covenants define expectations, measures of accountability and establish benchmarks. They should define a set of standards for communication, and problem solving and outline a chain of command. Do not assume that your children know what you expect of them—write it down and have both parties sign the document.

A family business council, is an effective tool for communicating to all family members, both those active and inactive in the business. This is the place where your family can be informed of your vision for succession, their roles in this process and what they can expect. The key is that you control this communication process through the use of an experienced succession planner trained in family dynamics and communication facilitation.

9. Family Governance

Employment in a family business is an opportunity, not a birthright.

Family members are role models for employees. However, non-family employees can resent family members for a casual "personal property" attitude towards business personnel and equipment. Through developing a unity of opinion and adherence to agreements regarding such things as family member compensation and perks, there is substantially less vulnerability to bad attitudes by employees or friction among family members.

The key to governance is that family members need to fully understand that they are always under a microscope and that employees expect them to take advantage of their family position. Therefore, in order for family members to gain the respect necessary to one day lead the company, they will need to work harder than non-family members and have a good attitude. Hard work is easy for employees to measure. An attitude that conveys, "I'm a team player and I'm willing to help you succeed," will cause employees to help the family member succeed since he or she is the future of the company. In contrast, an attitude of entitlement, "I'm the boss' son or daughter, therefore I can do what I want," is the kiss of death with employees who could take delight in throwing an heir-do-well under the perception bus. To avoid these pitfalls, develop written, detailed expectations so that everything is clear to family members and supervising managers.

10. Owner Motivation and Perspective

Many times a business owner will view the business as, "What can it do for me?" This attitude can trickle down and negatively affect the stewardship responsibility of business owners to their employees, management and community. A business will take on the personality of the business owner and can either be a positive force and attract good people and business or a negative force and slowly discourage business and a productive work environment. Additionally, although they are very successful by being willing to make the hard decisions, business owners must be open to the suggestions and concerns of the management team they have built. Essentially, an important attitude is that the owner understands that his success is the by-product of the collaboration of others, that he or she is the servant, always sensitive to the needs of employees, managers and the community.

Motivation of a business owner is also critical to the succession of a business. Unless a business owner understands that there is an appropriate time to step aside and transfer ownership and control, there will never be succession. Developing an exit strategy is important to allow the successor time to learn and make mistakes while the business owner is still accessible. This can be one of the most difficult steps for a business owner to be willing to take, but it is crucial to succession. Space must be created and successors and managers must develop the ability to make the critical decisions you have made that are necessary for the productive continuance of the business.

So, what is the current status of your succession planning? The Succession Success Analysis on the facing page will give you the opportunity to grade your business's odds of succeeding through the next generation.

From a succession planning perspective, assuming Vital Success Factors (the ones in bold) are scored at 8 or higher, we feel an index of 90 percent or above generally reflects the Success Margin that will provide the marketing momentum, management resilience, financial strength and administrative preparation to carry the business through the challenge of ownership and management transition.

If you don't have a family successor who is ready, willing and able, what alternatives do you have to selling?

Are you in control of what happens with your business? As stated earlier, most business owners want to be in control. Unless you have successfully addressed the issues discussed in this chapter, as represented by achieving a score of 90 percent or above on the Succession Success Analysis, you are not in control and the odds are stacked against succession for your company. Selling the business is a viable succession alternative and this may be the course you need to take. But when and how to achieve a successful sale is often difficult due to the business owner's reluctance to sell and then face the issue, "now, what do I do with my time and energy?" If you don't have a family successor who is ready, willing and able, what alternatives do you have to selling?

Succession Bridges™ [1]

Often, a business owner will fail to create a plan to bridge the gap until a family member is qualified, or in the absence of qualified family members. The creation of this plan allows the business owner to sell when ready while maximizing management talents and protecting the value of the business for the family. It is also a career retention incentive for managers. This process is important for business owners who do not want to sell their business, but do not have qualified successors. It is also for those owners who are without successors and who want to sell part of their business to key managers. It is also designed for those owners who want to sell at a predetermined point in the future or for those who simply want a back-up plan. It's a plan that involves highly motivated, capable manag-

---

[1] Succession Bridge™ is a customized financial and management package developed by The Rawls Group that provides a management continuity bridge for owners.

The Rawls Group Succession Success℠ Analysis

Success Factor	Potential	Position	Comments
Mission Statement	10		Has this been defined and written down?
Management and/or Growth Vision	10		Has your vision been developed and shared with management?
Strategic Plan with Accountability Steps	10		Is there a detailed plan with specific action steps?
Personal Financial Planning	10		How much of your net worth is tied to your business? The higher the percentage, the lower your score.
Exit Strategy	10		Has an exit strategy been developed and communicated?
Bsns Location/Facilities	10		Are you in the right facility and location for the next 15-20 yrs?
Business Community	10		Is your community thriving or will you need to move eventually?
Business Structure	10		How is your business structured? S-corp & LLC are more flexible for succession than C-corp.
Business Documentation	10		Are stockholders/partnership agreements up-to-date?
Manufacturer	10		Does the manufacturer have a positive relationship with your successor?
Product Diversification	10		Are you a single point vs. diversified?
Business Capitalization	10		Over-capitalized can cause loose business practices. Too, under-capitalized can create problems.
Business Profitability	10		Goal for succession is profits in excess of industry standards.
Community Involvement	10		Especially important in smaller communities. Some owners can be over-involved at the expense of running the business.
Successor Management Talent	10		Do the successors have what it takes with experience and training?
Successor Management Experience	10		How much experience do the successors have in the overall running of the business?
Successor Owner Training	10		Have the successors received formal training in the business?
Successor Management Confidence	10		Does the successor believe he/she can do it? Give me the ball!
Supporting Management Talents	10		How capable are your key managers?
Supporting Management Experience	10		How experienced are your key managers?
Management Synergy	10		How effective is your management team at maximizing productivity and profitability of the business?
Customer Satisfaction	10		How do you fare on CSI Scores?
Family Involvement	10		Is family a plus or minus in your business?
Family Harmony	10		How well do they support each other in the business and have they been tested under duress?
Employee Satisfaction	10		Employee retention and enthusiasm or are they coasting?
Credit Continuity	10		How much debt do you have and how will your lenders feel if they have to deal with your children or someone else if you are no longer available?
Franchise Continuity	10		Is your successor documentation completed and accepted by the manufacturers?
Estate Documentation	10		Is your estate plan in place and reviewed annually?
Probate Avoidance	10		Have assets been re-titled and trusts set up to avoid probate?
Estate Tax Financing	10		Is liquidity available and a plan in place to pay the estate tax without it adversely affecting the business?
Family Understanding of Estate Plans	10		Have you met with your family and described what will happen to avoid family disharmony?
Owner Humility	10		How open are you to succession ideas and to being challenged regarding the family and business issues which need to be addressed to achieve Succession Success?
Totals	320		

ers and/or family members who are seeking career opportunities and are willing to go the extra mile.

Your business is your legacy and succession is worth the effort! By now you understand that to commit to succession success involves significant time, energy, finances and a willingness to come out of your comfort zone by addressing issues that may be uncomfortable, especially when it involves family. But, your business is your life's work and the rewards of seeing your legacy continue for the benefit of your family, management, employees and your community is worth the effort. As one business owner said, "To watch my children succeed in my business is the greatest joy of my life."

Retirement, whether in a total sense or "entrepreneurial retirement" should involve peace of mind knowing that your life's work and legacy are protected. When done properly and all the pertinent issues have been addressed, succession planning results in peace of mind.

 **Hugh B. Roberts**, CFP®, Partner, The Rawls Group / Family Business Resource Center, is a Certified Financial Planner™. He has been involved in working with business owners nationwide, regarding their estate and business succession planning since 1982. Mr. Roberts has a B.A. from the University of Colorado and an M.A. from Fuller Seminary.

Hugh specializes in dealing with the issues that must be resolved by business owners and their families in order to preserve assets and develop succession plans for their businesses. Working in concert with the clients' other advisors, he orchestrates the development of an integrated plan addressing the business, tax, financial, family and emotional issues that must be overcome to ensure the preservation of businesses, estates and families. In the past 15 years, Hugh has spoken to the AICPA, Young Presidents Organization (YPO), 60 Automotive Twenty-Groups, multiple state Auto Dealers Associations, and is a frequently invited speaker at many national business owner conventions. Hugh is currently working with clients in 43 states nationwide.

Hugh Roberts can be reached at: The Rawls Group, 21031 Ventura Blvd, Suite 704, Woodland Hills, CA 91364; (tel) 818.610.3480; (email) hbroberts@rawlsgroup.com; (website) www.rawlsgroup.com and www.seekingsuccession.com.

Finding a Qualified Professional for
Wealth Management and Preservation

Ira G. Rapaport, President
New England Private Wealth Advisors

Selecting a good financial advisor should not be left to chance. Your personal financial future depends on the financial advice you rely upon. Within the United States, alone, several hundred thousand people call themselves financial advisors, each with different levels of experience and competence. Unfortunately, "financial advisor" is a generic term and is applied to insurance agents, stockbrokers, financial planners, wealth managers, bankers, and a number of others. Because of the potential for confusion, it is important to know how to identify and select the right advisor for your particular situation and goals, and avoid the common investment pitfalls.

The goal of this chapter is to help you recognize the important areas to research and to help you learn the right questions to ask a prospective advisor. If you are informed, you will be in a better position to select an appropriate advisor—one that can provide you a high level of advice and help you attain your financial and life objectives.

Recommendations

Finding the right financial advisor is as important as finding a qualified doctor to treat a specific medical condition. For example, if you need a heart operation, you would seek a highly qualified cardiologist with a history of success in the specific type of surgery you require. Even if a friend knew of a good cardiologist, you would still want to check on the doctor's reputation, credentials, history of successful operations, etc. The same should

be true of financial advisors. It is not enough to rely solely on the recommendations from friends and family members, chance meetings at
a social gatherings, or advertisements. Qualified recommendations
usually can come from other professionals who work in the financial
industry, such as insurance agents, estate planning attorneys, accountants, etc. While this can serve as a starting point, it is important that
you conduct your own research and due diligence.

Your Personal Goals and Objectives

Prior to meeting or selecting a financial advisor, you should identify your own goals and expectations. It is important to find an advisor who will tailor his or her services to your needs and desires, and
within your personal constraints such as time horizon, risk tolerance,
and long-term objectives. Write down your goals using as much detail as possible. This will help clarify your thinking and become the
framework of your initial meetings with financial advisor candidates.
A qualified financial advisor will help you refine those goals even
further, extensively explore your needs, and invest the time to learn
about you as a person prior to formulating a plan to help you achieve
your goals.

Once you have clearly identified your goals, it is time to research
and create a list of prospective advisors to interview. Include the
names of possible candidates from friends, family, and other professionals you know. Contact the offices of candidate advisors and
schedule an initial interview. Consider making the time to interview a few candidates before making a final selection. You and your
spouse may prefer to bring a trusted friend with investment experience. Ultimately, you should select someone you feel comfortable
with; however, your trusted friend may be able to assist you in asking questions and interpreting answers.

During the interview process, be aware of advisors who do not
actively try to understand your goals, who promise high stock market
performance, and do not take copious notes. Good advisors will want
a comprehensive understanding of your financial and nonfinancial
goals and objectives.

This chapter will provide questions to ask during the interviews
which will help you get a better understanding of the advisor's competence, integrity, commitment to ethical behavior and his or her adherence to high professional standards. The advisor should be a good
listener, put your needs and interests first, and accept a level of fiduciary responsibility for the decisions made. Ultimately, you'll need
complete confidence and trust in that person.

Certain questions to ask and areas to explore with your financial

The Total Picture

At the end of the day it is what you keep, not what you make, that counts. If you are paying a lot of taxes your investment profits may be minimized. Situations such as those in the sidebar on page 148 highlight the need for comprehensive financial advice and for a qualified financial planner to look at your overall situation to notice important areas that other specialists may have overlooked.

Specialists (CPA, attorneys, stockbrokers, etc.) may not recognize certain opportunities because they are not trained in certain financial areas. They may view things from a particular perspective, and not necessarily from the ideal perspective for your particular situation. While they may do an excellent job in their area of expertise, they may not be able to suggest an optimal solution.

Financial planning and financial advice should take into account distinct areas including: retirement, charitable and estate planning, taxes, and investments.

A financial advisor should coordinate and integrate all areas to fully optimize your wealth. Advisors' roles are often that of a liaison with other professionals in your life. A financial advisor will have a broad familiarity with different financial disciplines and can coordinate the activities of these professionals to provide you the best options.

advisor candidates can be divided into four primary areas:

1. Core values and competencies
2. Services
3. Compensation
4. Regulatory compliance

Core Values and Competencies Questions

The answers to these questions will help you identify an advisor who has the skills, experience, and team that are necessary for success. Realize that there is no right or wrong answer. The advisor's attitude and willingness to provide comprehensive answers will provide you with a wealth of information. Remember, you may be placing your financial future in this person's hands, so asking these types of questions is imperative.

What is your educational background?

In addition to a college degree, a qualified financial advisor will have advanced education in such topics as investment management, financial planning, wealth management, taxes, insurance, and/or estate planning. Since no one individual can know everything, it is important to find an advisor who has a team of experts that he or she can access, experts who have knowledge in various financial disciplines. Ideally, an advisor should be using a team approach and have a built-in infrastructure allowing the advisor to tap into the expertise of others.

A qualified advisor should regularly participate in continuing education programs to stay on top of industry changes and trends. Timely knowledge, especially in such areas as investments, law and taxation, is essential.

What are your financial planning credentials/designations and affiliations?

There is a number of professional certifications or designations that financial advisors can attain. For example, I am a Certified Public Accountant (CPA), Certified Financial Planner™ (CFP®), Accredited Investment Fiduciary (AIF), Certified Investment Management Analyst (CIMA), Personal Financial Specialist (PFS), and have a master's degree in taxation. As a result, I am required to constantly hone my skills and increase my knowledge.[1] Your advisor should do the same.

You will want to choose an advisor who has designations or credentials matching your needs and not choose an advisor merely because he or she has "alphabet soup" behind his or her name. Ask the candidate advisor how one or more of the designations apply to your particular situation. You should receive a clear, concise explanation. You may also want to verify that the advisor is an active member of the organizations issuing the credentials. A simple web search will enable you to contact the organization and confirm the advisor is active.

How long have you been offering financial planning or investment management services?

An advisor with one or more designations does not mean that he or she is a competent and qualified advisor. You want to work with an advisor who has *"relevant experience,"* an individual who works with people in a similar situation as yourself. For example, if you are a retired executive or approaching retirement, you may need help with stock option decisions and planning. An advisor who has helped other corporate executives with stock options should be aware of specific financial considerations and tactics that you, or an inexperienced advisor, may not have taken into consideration.

Carefully examine the advisor's background and experience. If you have a complicated financial situation, you will want to find an individual who has been in the financial services industry for a significant period of time and provides comprehensive financial planning or wealth management. (This will be discussed in greater detail later.)

Will you provide me with references from other professionals?

Learn as much as possible about the advisor, as well as the associated firm's abilities, strategies, and reputation from a third party within the financial services industry. Highly competent financial advisors should be able to provide you with a comprehensive list of references upon request. When you call references, questions such as: How long have

---

[1] For more information on the most recognized designations, visit www.nasd.org. Search for "designations," Select "Understanding Investment Professional Designations." Select the printer-friendly chart.

you known the advisor? How do you collaborate on client cases? How often are you in contact with this advisor? Are there other advisors that you might recommend instead? Do you refer your clients to this advisor? Would you use this person as your own personal financial advisor? If not, why not? Answers to these types of questions, from three or four of the referred professionals, will provide excellent insight into the capabilities of your candidate advisor.

It is equally, if not more important, to ask the prospective advisor for a list of client references that you can call. Of course, the advisor will give you names of clients who are satisfied with the services provided. However, you can ask the client such questions as: How often does the advisor call you or meet with you to review your financial situation? Is the advisor easily accessible? What differentiates this advisor from other financial advisors you have worked with? Does the financial advisor work well with the other professionals you currently work with?

Consider telling the client referrals something about your own personal situation and let them tell you if they are in a similar situation. This will help you find an advisor with relevant experience to your particular situation so you can benefit from the experience that the advisor has gained from working with people in similar situations.

To return to the previous doctor analogy, if you needed a heart operation you would want a surgeon who has successfully performed numerous identical heart operations. You would not go to a general practitioner or to a cancer specialist.

How many clients do you work with?

As a client, you need to get personalized attention, and do not want to be just another number. The number of clients an advisor works with is an indication of how much attention he or she will devote to you. If the number of clients seems high, ask how advising that many clients is possible and how much individual attention you can expect to receive.

Also ask how often the advisor meets with each client, what type of service can be expected, whether or not the financial advisor or a team member is going to be providing that service, the names of the other individuals you will be interacting with, etc. You should meet these individuals and understand who will be your direct point of contact.

Are you currently engaged in any other business?

Some financial advisors wear many hats. In fact, some actually work as a financial advisor on a part-time basis. Clearly you want a full-time, professional financial advisor.

Do you work as an independent or with a national/recognized firm?

An advisor who is associated with a national firm can have numerous benefits such as extensive resources and research. However, a single practitioner may be able to focus better on your specific needs. You should realize that an advisor who is working with certain firms may not be able to offer or manage certain financial instruments. Such advisors may not have as much independence or objectivity as you would like.

Do you have a business continuity plan?

In the event that the advisor retires, passes away, has an accident, or transitions out of the financial services business, what will happen to you and your financial plan or investments? You should be looking for lifetime relationships—ideally an advisory team that can work with multiple generations. While multiple-generation planning is not absolutely necessary, the advisor should have the appropriate infrastructure to take care of various contingencies.

Services Questions

The following series of questions will help you determine the level of service and advice that the financial advisor can offer. More choices lead to greater flexibility and additional opportunities. If the advisor has only three or four investment products in his or her universe, your opportunities are considerably limited. On the other hand, be wary of the individual advisor who claims he or she can do absolutely everything. In such cases, inquire about the credentials of the supporting team.

Is there an information-gathering process in place to learn about your clients?

The advisor should have a standard process to gather necessary information about you. A data-gathering form contains basic information such as address, Social Security number, date of birth, etc. This form should also include personal data about you and your family, employment and business information, and any other advisors you are working with.

An advisor should ask you to complete a risk tolerance questionnaire. The information you enter on this worksheet and your reactions to certain investment scenarios should be instrumental in determining an appropriate portfolio. An advisor should also initiate discussions to really get to know you personally.

Do you offer assistance with the plan implementation?

Realize that a financial plan has little value if it is not implemented. Search for an advisor who can "help you make it happen." Otherwise, you may be forced to use an entirely different advisor who may not have the capability to execute.

Do you offer continuous, ongoing advice regarding my financial affairs, including advice on non-investment related issues?

A financial advisor should contact you two to four times a year and review your goals, discuss how the plan is working, and update himself or herself on your personal and financial situation. For example, the birth of a child may require updating a will, adding a beneficiary, obtaining additional insurance, and creating a college fund. Marriage or divorce can also trigger major changes to a financial plan. You should make your financial advisor aware of a change, or the possibility of a change, in your circumstances. A good advisor-client relationship is based on clear, open communication.

Explore all of the ways in which you and your advisor can communicate. For example, are you allowed to contact the advisor via e-mail or telephone at any time? Do you have an emergency number for the advisor? Does the advisor offer newsletters and client education seminars?

Other than receiving my permission to debit my investment account for your fee, do you take custody of, or will you have access to, my assets?

Ask about how the assets are insured or protected and about other safeguards. Where will the assets actually be held? Who is the custodian?

If you were to provide me ongoing investment advisory services, do you require "discretionary" trading authority over my investment accounts?

Discretionary authority allows advisors to place trading orders without consulting you. Depending upon your personal situation and/or comfort level, you may or may not wish to be involved with every transaction and decision.

Make sure that you understand the advisor's investment philosophy and strategy and that you are comfortable with his or her approach. Regardless of whether or not you grant discretionary authority, you should continually monitor the activity within your investment accounts.

Compensation Questions

An important question to ask is, ***"How does the advisor get paid?"*** Within the financial services industry there is a variety of compensation methods used by individual advisors and their firms. No one particular method is intrinsically better or worse than another. The most popular methods include: fee-only, commissions, retainer, hourly charges, a percentage of assets under management, or some combination of the above.

Many investors are comfortable with the fee-only approach because the financial advisor or financial planner is offering an investment *process,* not simply a potpourri of unrelated investment *products.* The fee-only ap-

The Benefits of Having a Financial Planner and Getting Comprehensive Advice

I believe that affluent and/or wealthy individuals should insist upon a financial planner or wealth manager who offers comprehensive advice. Otherwise, you may be missing out on many important planning opportunities. The following series of examples highlights the benefits of working with an advisor who is able to look at the big picture.

Below are some common situations that I regularly encounter.

• Clients are eligible for a Roth IRA, but their CPA is either focused on taxes or not knowledgeable about this opportunity. A good financial planner may see that the client is eligible for a conversion.

• Many clients give away cash instead of appreciated securities for charitable commitments. Some advisors are so focused on investments that they may miss many planning opportunities that would otherwise save their clients taxes and/or a significant amount of money.

• A self-employed client can have a self-employed 401(K) plan and, therefore, is able to make much larger contributions. Unfortunately, many such clients are still only using an IRA, which severely limits the amount of the contribution.

• Many clients are in an alternative minimum tax (AMT) situation and do not realize that certain types of investments may allow them to maximize their opportunities.

• Clients have advisors who have not reviewed their tax returns for the last three years. A loss carry-forward can significantly alter the posture of an investment portfolio. Similarly, unrealized capital gains may require a different strategy. How can someone offer financial advice if they are not aware of the big picture?

• Clients who are divorced and remarried often forget to remove the previous spouse as a beneficiary.

proach best removes potential conflicts of interest that can be inherent in a commission relationship. However, there also are commissioned brokers who provide investment advice with the best interests of the client in mind.

Regardless of the compensation method employed by a financial advisor, you should receive a written engagement letter that outlines the fee structure and/or types of compensation the financial advisor will receive when working with you. There should be "full disclosure" or "transparency." It is important to realize that some financial advisors receive additional compensation from firms or investment product providers for selling certain products or services. Some advisors also pay or receive referral fees from attorneys, accountants, insurance agents, mortgage brokers, etc. Be aware that there may be a potential conflict of interest in these types of situations.

Do you have a minimum fee?

If you have limited financial planning needs and/or a small portfolio, paying a minimum fee may not be in your best interest. Instead you may wish to search for a flat fee or find an advisor who charges on an hourly basis.

Are you limited to presenting certain types of invest-

ments or investment products?

This question is similar to one posed earlier regarding limitations a firm may impose. Such limitations may preclude you from maximizing your investment opportunities. You are actually asking whether the advisor can provide you with a full range of solutions or merely the best solutions available to the advisor. There is a significant difference.

Are any investment expenses waived or reduced by employing you as my investment advisor?

Based upon your situation and relationship that the advisor has with the firms they are associated with, you may be able to receive certain discounts or arrange to have certain minimums waived or lowered. It is always in your best interest to ask.

Regulatory Compliance Questions

Needless to say, you want an ethical professional handing your money. Following are some of the questions to ask and some organizations that can help you answer them.

Have you ever been cited by a professional or regulatory governing body for disciplinary reasons?

If you are working with a broker or advisor, you can obtain a tremendous amount of information about the broker's or advisor's background by visiting www.nasd.com/brokercheck. The telephone number is 301-590-6500. If the broker or advisor has been sued, ask hard-nosed questions.

Additionally, federal and state laws require that certain firms—Registered Investment Advisors (RIA)—offering investment advisory services to the public be registered with either the U.S. Securities & Exchange Commission (SEC) or the regulatory agency within the state they do business. SEC Form ADV has two parts: Part I contains information about the advisor's business and whether he or she has had problems with regulators or clients. Part II outlines the advisor's services, fees, and strategies. Before you hire an advisor, always request and read both parts of the ADV. You can find Part I online. Visit www.sec.gov, or call the SEC at 202-942-7040 for additional information.

By law, Registered Investment Advisors owe a fiduciary duty to their clients. They are required to always act in good faith and with candor. They are also required to be proactive in disclosing any conflicts of interest.

The following websites and telephone numbers can help you in your search.

- **Certified Financial Planner Board of Standards, Inc.**
  Telephone: 888-237-6275   www.CFP.net

- **North American Securities Administration**
  Telephone: 202-737-0900   www.nasaa.org
- **National Association of Insurance Commissioners**
  Telephone: 816-842-3600   www.naic.org
- **National Association of Securities Dealers Regulation**
  Telephone: 800-289-9999   www.nasdr.com
- **Securities and Exchange Commission**
  Telephone: 202-942-7040   www.sec.gov

In Conclusion

Finding the right financial advisor is an important component to financial success and should not be left to chance. While getting recommendations from others is a good place to start, understand that you should be conducting your own due diligence. Remember to ask numerous questions before you place your money, and possibly your financial future, into someone else's hands. You want to ensure that the advisor's qualifications, personality, and goals match yours. You want to trust that advisor. Above all, you should feel confident AND comfortable with the professional whom you choose to control your financial future.

Ira G. Rapaport, CPA/PFS, CIMA, CFP®, MST, AIF, is CEO of New England Private Wealth Advisors, LLC (NEPWA). NEPWA is an independent, fee-only, financial planning, wealth management and registered investment advisory firm. Ira has been providing a broad range of customized and comprehensive investment consulting and financial planning services for more than 20 years.

NEPWA provides unbiased and tailored advice to each client in a disciplined and thoughtful manner. They take an innovative and highly personalized approach to integrate financial planning solutions with client investment portfolios. They service a diverse, high net worth client base, including professionals, retirees, widows/widowers, divorcées/divorcés and business owners.

Ira can be reached at New England Private Wealth Advisors, LLC, 36 Washington Street, Suite 395; Wellesley, MA 02481; (tel) 781.416.1701; (email) ira@nepwealth.com.

Ira would like to thank his entire team for their valuable contributions to the creation and development of this chapter.

Your Life:
Living the Retirement Of Your Dreams

Steve Vernon, President
Rest-of-Life Communications

"How much money do I need?" People frequently ask me this question when they hear I'm a consulting actuary who writes and speaks on retirement issues. Until recently, I would give the conventional advice: "You need a retirement income equaling 60-90 percent of your pay just before retirement, and to generate that kind of income, you need a gazillion dollars." I found that this answer doesn't work for most people. They simply don't have the kind of retirement savings needed to replace their standard of living they enjoyed while working.

So, I've gone on a quest in search of a better answer. I'll share what I've learned so far, and will point you to some good resources (included in the Additional Resources section at the back of the book) to help you find your answers.

But, back to the original question—now I ask a question in return. "What do you really want—retirement or happiness?" My intention is to trigger some reflection and creative thinking.

I realized that most of us really want happiness and fulfillment in our later years, and we think that retirement is the solution. Various surveys show that about half of all Americans are unhappy with their work, and would quit working tomorrow if they won the lottery. There are a number of reasons why people feel this way—pick one or more that might apply to you.

1. We don't like our work because:

- We're bored.
- We don't like our work environment – our boss, our customers, the immediate surroundings, etc.
- We're tired of the commute and daily grind.
- Work keeps us from things that we really want to do, and so on.

2. We're used up—we might have poor health and can't continue working.

3. Our culture sends us powerful messages—that retirement is the right way to finish our life, that we're being cheated out of life if we can't retire.

So, *not working* is the ticket to happiness and fulfillment, right?

Well, not so fast. I'm taking a deeper look in my quest.

Moving Beyond 'Not Being Unhappy'

First, there are two aspects to being happy and fulfilled:

1. Not being unhappy, and

2. Finding what makes you happy and fulfilled.

You might ask, "What's the difference?" There's a big difference—we might have different items on each list. If work makes us unhappy and we stop working, then all we've done is remove our source of unhappiness. We haven't found what makes us happy and fulfilled. However, I don't want to diminish the importance of removing our sources of unhappiness. It's a good first step, but we're not done.

The trouble is, many of us don't think much beyond *not working* when we plan our retirement. That's when we run into problems. The most successful retirees retire *to* a life that is rich with good relationships and activities; they think well beyond retiring *from* work.

Items on the *not-being-unhappy* list include mitigating or preventing the following:

- Poor relationships with friends and family
- Things going poorly for the important people in our lives
- Not having enough money to meet our basic needs
- Poor health
- Boredom and loneliness
- Not being useful or needed
- The perception that others have more than we do, and/or
- The feeling that we've been cheated out of life or have been treated unfairly

Challenges specific to retirement include the lack of social contacts provided by work, and the unrealistic reliance on our spouse to fulfill all our emotional needs (translated: too much time with our spouse).

Any one of these things can make us unhappy. However, once we re-move the source of unhappiness, we may take it for granted. Health is one example. I'm certainly unhappy when I'm sick, and I'm very happy when I recover—for awhile. Then, as time progresses, I take my good health for granted. Being healthy is no longer a source of happiness. I don't wake up every morning saying 'thank goodness I'm healthy.' (However, one school of thought urges us to count our blessings frequently, and research shows that this act will make us happier.)

Many chapters in this book focus on generating financial security—having enough money in retirement. Clearly this is necessary to avoid unhappiness about money, and is an important part of our life plan. But, by itself, this won't make us happy and fulfilled.

So, it's important to mitigate, avoid or prevent things that make us un-happy. But now let's move beyond this, to the second aspect of happiness and fulfillment that I mentioned previously.

It's important to focus on what will make
you happy and fulfilled in your later years,
and then build the financial resources
to support the life you want.

It's important to focus on what will make you happy and fulfilled in your later years, and then build the financial resources to support the life you want. These financial resources can include all the things discussed in this book—401(k) and IRA accounts, pensions, Social Security—but they can also include income from continued work.

First, let's give a definition. When I say happy and fulfilled, I'm not talk-ing about the good feelings that come from going out to eat, watching a good movie, or buying something you really want. The psychologists call this moment-to-moment happiness, which is different from deep satisfaction with life. Here's one example of this. If you ask a young parent who is up at midnight with a sick child if they are happy at that moment, you might get an angry stare. But, that same parent might say that raising a child is one of the most enjoyable and meaningful things they are doing with their life.

In retirement, most of us want a healthy balance of both moment-to-mo-ment happiness and deep fulfillment with life. Our culture focuses mostly on moment-to-moment happiness. TV, radio, and print advertisements tell us that we'll be happy if we take the exotic vacation, play golf, and buy lots of stuff. However, this leaves most of us with empty feelings if that's all we do.

What Makes You Truly Happy?

It turns out that psychologists and social researchers have spent a lot of time recently researching what makes people happy and fulfilled. More specifically for our purposes, they have focused on the question "does money buy happiness?" We can get valuable insight from this research that will help us answer the original question—"How much money do we need?"

Research[1] shows that the following makes us happy and fulfilled:

- Having good relationships with family and friends, and healing issues that need healing.
- Pursuing our passions, interests, hobbies.
- Doing our life's work. Many of us find deep satisfaction from working on a challenge.
- Being productive and engaged with life. Applying our skills and experience in a way that is consistent with our interests and values.
- Continuing to learn and grow.
- Appreciating beauty in the world—art, music, the outdoors.
- Contributing to the greater good of our community, country or the world—something larger than ourselves. Creating our legacy.

Which of these resonate with you? How much money do we need for these things?

With respect to happiness and money, a number of studies[2] show that if we don't have enough money to meet our basic needs, then we might be unhappy. Adding more money does increase our happiness. But once we meet our basic needs, adding extra money doesn't add much to our happiness, as we mentioned earlier.

So here's one answer to the "how much money do we need" question —just enough to meet our basic human needs.

But, how do we define these basic human needs? Some people would say it's a roof over our heads, safe environment, necessary medical care, and food on the table. Millions of people around the world would be quite happy with just this. Many Americans would classify items as necessities that others around the world would call luxuries: cars, TVs, a nicely furnished house, and cellphones are all examples.

---

[1] *The Dubious Rewards of Consumption*, by Alan Thein Durning, the *New Renaissance Magazine* Vol. 3, No. 3; *How Much is Enough?* The Consumer Society and the Future of the Earth (WW Norton & Company, 1992); 2005 Happiness Study, GfK Roper Reports Worldwide Survey; Survey, August, 2006 edition of *Money Magazine*; Can Money Buy Happiness?; CNNMoney. com, July 18, 2006.
[2] Survey, August 2006 edition, *Money Magazine*; Can Money Buy Happiness?, CNNMoney.com, July 18, 2006; also appears in *The Good Life and Its Discontents*, Robert Samuelson; *Authentic Happiness*, Martin Seligman (Free Press, 2002)

Here's where the research provides more fascinating insights. It turns out that most people's happiness with respect to money and consumption is *relative*.[3] That is, if we have about as much money and stuff as our peers, then we're happy; however, if we feel like others have a lot more than we do, we're unhappy.

One study reported in *Psychological Science in the Public Interest* magazine, shows the respondents from the Forbes list of the 400 richest Americans and the Maasai of East Africa were almost equally satisfied and ranked relatively high in well-being. Some people might think this is proof that money and consumption don't buy happiness. However, what it really shows is when a typical Maasai compares himself or herself to peers, they feel about the same as when a wealthy American does the same. Most Americans would be unhappy with the Maasai lifestyle, but if it's what everybody else has, then life's not so bad.

I found another body of research[4] that illustrates this phenomenon. Americans report themselves to be about as happy today as they were 10, 20, 30, 40 and 50 years ago. But we consume five times as much stuff today as 50 years ago. Back then, people managed to be happy without the latest car, TV and DVDs, cellphones, computers, the Internet—things we take for granted today. Consuming more hasn't added to American's reported happiness.

So what does all this prove? That it is *possible* to be happy with not much stuff—the problems come when we compare ourselves to others, or compare our current situation to the past.

Now, let's turn to working during our later years.

Working in Retirement – Oxymoron or Good Idea?

I found some interesting insights in something as mundane as a mortality study conducted by the Society of Actuaries.[5] First, it looked at death rates among healthy men between ages 50 and 70. The men who were working had about half the death rates of men who weren't working. The effect was there for women, but not as pronounced.

What's going on—why are workers healthier and living longer? Is this causation (work enables us to be healthier) or correlation (it's just a coincidence)? I looked deeper and found a few studies[6] that weigh in on the

[3] The Dubious Rewards of Consumption, Alan Thein Durning, *New Renaissance Magazine* Vol. 3, No. 3; *How Much is Enough? The Consumer Society and the Future of the Earth* (WW Norton & Company, 1992), this article cites several studies supporting this phenomenon; *Relative Income and Happiness: Are Americans on a Hedonistic Treadmill?* Glenn Firegaugh, Pennsylvania State University, Laura Tach, Harvard University; Can Money Buy Happiness?, CNNMoney.com, July 18, 2006; Psychological Science in the Public Interest, September, 2004

[4] IBID; Can Money Buy Happiness? CNNMoney.com, July 18, 2006; *Psychological Science in the Public Interest*, Fall, 2004; The Keys to Happiness, and Why We Don't Use Them, LiveScience, February 27, 2006; *Authentic Happiness*, by Martin Seligman (Free Press, 2002)

[5] Society of Actuaries RP-2000 Mortality Study

[6] Individual Consequences of Volunteer and Paid Work in Old Age: Health and Mortality, by Ming-Ching Luoh and A. Regula Jerzog, *Journal of Health and Social Behavior 43* (December 2002); Dog Aging and Cognition Project, University of Toronto and University of California; *Successful Aging*, by John W. Rowe and Robert L. Kahn (DTP Health, 1998); *Aging Well*, by George Valliant (Little, Brown and Company, 2002)

causation side. Actually, what I found is that people who are actively engaged with life—who have powerful reasons for getting up in the morning—are healthier and live longer. Working can provide this engagement in life, but other activities can provide this as well.

Another aspect of the mortality study looked at income levels and mortality. People between ages 50 and 70 who had incomes above poverty levels had significantly lower death rates than people with incomes below the poverty level. This is consistent with other findings reported in this chapter—people meeting their basic human needs.

All this tells me that working in our later years isn't the curse that our culture portrays. It might not be so bad if it keeps us engaged in life and provides sufficient income to meet our needs. And it might get us health insurance through our employers—a valuable bonus!

This leads me to what I call the part-time math.

- Conventional wisdom on an adequate retirement income is 60% to 90% of our pay just before retirement. Well, if we work three days a week, that's 60% of our full-time pay, and four days a week is 80%. Maybe we should try working part-time to see if we can live on this conventional wisdom, before retiring completely. If we can't live on this income, maybe we're not ready for retirement. However, we might find this works just fine.

- For full-time workers, we spend five days per week getting ready for work, commuting, working, and recovering at the end of the day. We have two days left to ourselves. One of these days is typically spent on chores and errands. We really only have about one day to pursue our interests and passions. If we only work four days a week, we double the number of days to pursue our interests, and if we only work three days a week, we triple these days.

I've talked with a number of people who are working part time in their later years, and they say that they can see themselves living this way indefinitely. They have a sustainable life—one without a finish line. Many working Americans have a finish-line mentality—they're hanging on until the day they can retire and finally be happy. But if they take a realistic look at the financial resources needed to cross the finish line, the line gets pushed back many years. A source for unhappiness! Why not create a sustainable life *now*?

A Realistic, Healthy Life Plan

Let me put this all together for a healthy, realistic life plan. Here is a sample you can use as a personal template:

- I'll look for part-time work to bring in just enough money to meet my needs, when combined with my financial resources. I'll find work that I like, a safe working environment, respect from my peers and supervisors, social contacts, and the opportunity for continued learning and growth.

- I'm writing my own story about what makes me happy and fulfilled. I'll turn off the TV and tune out messages from our culture that don't work for me. Buying lots of stuff doesn't make me happy. TV ads intentionally try to give me the feeling that everybody else is buying their stuff, and I'm left out of the 'in' crowd if I don't go along. Bah! Instead, I'll build good relationships with family and friends, take care of my health, look for ways to be productive, and take the time to appreciate beauty in the world.

- If I do spend money on consumer items, I'll look for things that bring people together—that enhance my relationships with family and friends.

- I won't compare what I have to what others have. I'll make sure that many of my peers are in the same boat. Being surrounded by people who have more stuff than I have is a ticket to misery. If I'm fortunate enough to have more than others, instead of being a source of envy, I'll share my good fortune and spread the wealth to help family, friends and community.

- Everybody has a history of emotional wounds and unfairness. Some of these can be quite painful, and need the proper acknowledgement and respect for healing. However, if I dwell on these, I'll only perpetuate my misery. Instead, I'll learn what I can, move on with my life, count my blessings, and nurture a positive attitude. I'll heed Abraham Lincoln's words—"Most people are as happy as they make up their minds to be."

- I'll work on my legacy to my children, friends, family, community, and the world.

With respect to this last item, I found a powerful exercise in a good book—*A Primer in Positive Psychology*,[7] by Christopher Peterson. It urges us to write our own obituary—and then live up to it. Try it!

Not only will this life plan give you a good chance for happiness and fulfillment, it has financial implications as well. Medical and scientific research shows that your physical health is affected by your emotional health. Also, diet, exercise and stress management significantly affects your physical health. You'll spend less on medical bills if you're happy and take care of yourself. Continued learning is an effective way to stave off dementia and Alzheimer's disease in your later years. And, you'll need good health if you want to continue working part time. So, investing in your happiness and health is an important part of your financial plan!

All of this might sound great, but it's easier said than done. Many of

---

[7] 2006, published by Oxford University Press

us need to change lifelong living habits, and it doesn't happen overnight or without effort. Facts and figures give insights that help, but that's not enough to motivate you to change. Building a positive image of a great *rest-of-life* is a powerful motivator. Pay attention to the good emotions, feelings and experiences that you want. It works better than fear of a lonely, unhealthy retirement, although a little fear can also be a healthy motivator. Another great help is to talk with friends and family who are facing the same challenges. It helps to hold hands and do it together!

Now Is The Time...

As you read in other chapters of this book, it takes time and effort to create the financial resources needed for a happy retirement. You need to invest an equal amount of time, effort and money into your health and happiness—it doesn't happen automatically.

We have strong, human needs to fit in, to be social, to love and be loved, and to be productive. These needs don't stop at retirement. In fact, they can increase in importance, particularly if we've neglected these needs in our past.

Now is the time to take care of ourselves, our family and friends. It's our time to take care of unfinished business, to do what calls to us. If we're feeling used up by work, the answer isn't to become useless, but instead look for continued ways to be useful. Find those powerful reasons for getting up in the morning.

Do I have a better answer to the original question? I think so. I'll build just enough financial resources to support the life that's best for my happiness, health and wealth. And I hope you can do the same. Otherwise, you better start working on saving your first gazillion!

◆◆◆

 **Steve Vernon** integrates two practices with his *rest-of-life* writing, seminars and workshops, which creates a holistic approach, 1) 31 years of financial analysis and research as a consulting actuary, including two books on retirement issues; and, 2) 15 years studying human potential, including attaining a 3rd degree black belt in aikido.

Steve is president of *Rest-of-Life* Communications, and an executive faculty member and research fellow with the California Institute of Finance at California Lutheran University. He retired recently as Vice President and Consulting Actuary with the influential human resources consulting firm Watson Wyatt Worldwide. For more than 31 years, Steve helped Fortune 500 companies design, administer, communicate and fund their retirement, benefits, and rewards programs. He has published three books with John Wiley & Sons, titled: *Employee Benefits: Valuation, Analysis and Strategies; Don't Work Forever!, Simple Steps Baby Boomers Must Take To Ever Retire;* and *Live Long & Prosper! Invest in Your Happiness, Health and Wealth for Retirement and Beyond.*

Steve is one of the most sought-after retirement experts in the country, and is quoted frequently in leading magazines and newspapers. He is an experienced speaker, with more than 220 presentations, keynote addresses and workshops on his books *Don't Work Forever!* and *Live Long & Prosper!* Steve graduated summa cum laude from the University of California, Irvine, with degrees in mathematics and social sciences. He lives in Oxnard California and can be reached at steve.vernon@restoflife.com.

Additional Resources

Chapter 1. Planing Your Retirement

- *Don't Work Forever! Simple Steps Baby Boomers Must Take To Ever Retire* by Steve Vernon (John Wiley & Sons, 1994)
- *Take Charge! A Woman's Guide to a Secure Retirement* by Edie Milligan (Alpha, 2001)
- *Baby Boomer Retirement* by Don Silver (Adams-Hall Publishing, 1998)
- *Everyone's Money Book on Retirement* by Jordan Goodman (Kaplan Business, 2002)*

Chapter 2. The Cost of Retirement

- *The Number: A Completely Different Way to Think About the Rest of Your Life* by Lee Eisenberg (Free Press, 2006)*
- *The Savage Number: How Much Money Do You Need to Retire?* by Terri Savage (John Wiley & Sons, 2005)*
- *It's More Than Money, It's Your LIfe: The New Money Club for Women* by Candace Bahr & Ginita Wall (John Wiley & Sons, 2003)

Chapter 3. Reverse Mortgages

- *The New Reverse Mortgage Formula: How to Convert Home Equity into Tax Free Income* by Tom Kelly (John Wiley & Sons, Inc. 2005)
- *The Power Years* by Ken Dychtwald (John Wiley & Sons, Inc, 2005)
- *The 7 Powers of Questions* by Dorothy Leeds (Berkley Publishing Group 2000)
- *How Not To Go Broke at 102* by Adriane Berg (John Wiley & Sons, Inc. 2004)

Chapter 4. Stocks, Bonds, Mutual Funds and Separate Accounts

- *Everyone's Money Book on Stocks, Bonds and Mutual Funds* by Jordan Goodman (Kaplan Business, 2002)*

Chapter 5. 401(k)s and IRAs

- *What You Ought to Know Before You Receive Your Retirement Distribution* by Tom Gau (MDP, 2006)
- *Parlay Your IRA into a Family Fortune* by Ed Slott (Penguin, 2005)

Chapters 8 and 9. Estate Planning

- *Estate Planning to Die For* by Sally Mulhern (Odyssey Press, 2006)*
- *A Parent's Guide to Wills and Trusts* by Don Silver (Adams-Hall Publishing, 1992)

Chapters 10 and 11. Charitable Giving

- *The Greater Good: How Philanthropy Drives the American Economy and Can Save Capitalism* by Claire Gaudiani (Owl Books, Henry Holt and Company, 2004)
- *Giving Wisely: Maximizing Your Charitable Giving* by Russ Alan Prince, Chris Blunt & Gary Rathbun (Oscar Printing Company, 2002)

---

* This book can be purchased at www.ffbookstore.com.

- *The Perfect Legacy: How to Establish Your Own Private Foundation* by Russ Alan Prince, Gary L. Rathbun & Karen Maru File (Hnw Pr, 1998)*
- www.advisorsinphilanthropy.com
- www.philanthropicwill.com

Chapter 12. Business Succession Planning

- *Seeking Succession: How to Continue the Family Business Legacy* by Loyd Rawls (Family Business Resource Center, 2004)
- *Your Golden Goose, The Family Business Council* by Loyd Rawls (Family Business Resource Center, 2006)
- *The Succession Bridge: Key Manager Succession Alternatives for Family-Owned Businesses* by Loyd Rawls (Family Business Resource Center, 2004)
- www.seekingsuccession.com
- www.rawlsgroup.com

Chapter 13. Finding a Qualified Professional

- *Sins of Omission: Things Your Broker Should be Telling You!* by Michael Kaselnak (Financial Forum Publishing, 2005)*
- *The Trust Equation: The Savvy Investor's Guide to Selecting a Competent, Ethical Financial Advisor* by Steven Drozdeck & Lyn Fisher (Financial Forum Publishing, 2005)*
- *Wealth Management Teams* by Steven Drozdeck & Lyn Fisher (Financial Forum Publishing, 2005)*

Chapter 14. Living the Retirement of Your Dreams

- *Aging Well* by George E. Valliant, M.D. (Little, Brown and Company, 2002)
- *Successful Aging* by John W. Rowe, M.D. and Robert L. Kahn, PhD (Bantam Doubleday Dell, 1999)
- *Authentic Happiness* by Martin Seligman (Nicholas Brealey Publishing, 2003)
- *The Art of Happiness* by the Dalai Lama and Dr. Howard Cutler (Putnam Publishing Group, 1998)
- *The Art of Happiness at Work* by the Dalai Lama and Dr. Howard Cutler (Hodder Mobius, UK, 2003)
- *If I Live to be 100* by Neenah Ellis (Random House, 2002)
- *The Soul of Money* by Lynne Twist (Sounds True, 2006)
- *A Primer in Positive Psychology* by Christopher Peterson (Oxford University Press, 2006)
- *The Retirement Activities Guide: Things to Do When Golf and Grandkids Aren't Enough* by Bruce Juell (3rd Age Press, 2006)
- *Don't Just Retire: Reformat!* by Dr. Lynda Falkenstein (2006)*
- *The New Retirementality* by Mitch Anthony (Kaplan Business, 2001)*
- *Live Long & Prosper! Invest in Your Happiness, Heath and Wealth for Retirement and Beyond* by Steve Vernon (John Wiley & Sons, 2004)*

---

* This book can be purchased at www.ffbookstore.com.

- *The Ultimate Gift* by Jim Stovall (RiverOak Publishing, 2001)*
- www.volunteermatch.org
- www.usafreedomcorps.gov
- www.charitynavigator.com
- www.pointsoflight.org
- www.retiresmiling.com

◆◆◆

---

* This book can be purchased at www.ffbookstore.com.

Index